Adna Brown

From Vermont to Damascus

Returning by Way of Beyrout, Smyrna, Ephesus, Athens...

Adna Brown

From Vermont to Damascus
Returning by Way of Beyrout, Smyrna, Ephesus, Athens...

ISBN/EAN: 9783744797757

Printed in Europe, USA, Canada, Australia, Japan

Cover: Foto ©Andreas Hilbeck / pixelio.de

More available books at **www.hansebooks.com**

FROM
VERMONT TO DAMASCUS

RETURNING BY WAY OF

BEYROUT, SMYRNA, EPHESUS, ATHENS, CONSTAN-
TINOPLE, BUDAPEST, VIENNA, PARIS,
SCOTLAND, AND ENGLAND

BY

ADNA BROWN

*With sixteen illustrations. Also, instructions how to prepare
for such a journey*

BOSTON
GEO. H. ELLIS, PRINTER, 141 FRANKLIN ST.
1895

TWO VERMONT LADIES.

PREFACE.

The urgent desires of the friends of the author of this volume that his Oriental letters should be compiled and put in book form prompted him to issue a work entitled "From Vermont to Damascus," taking the reader through the Oriental land, giving a vivid picture of the country, scenes, and people as he saw them from day to day, which was the richest experience of his life. Much has been added to these letters with illustrations,— directions for preparations for such a journey, value of the currency of different countries, etc.,— making the book a valuable one for persons intending to travel in a foreign land.

TABLE OF CONTENTS.

	PAGE
ON THE WAY TO NAPLES	3
LETTERS FROM ITALY . .	10
LETTERS FROM EGYPT . .	27
LETTERS FROM THE HOLY LAND .	66
LETTER FROM GREECE	138
LETTER FROM CONSTANTINOPLE . .	148
FROM CONSTANTINOPLE TO PARIS	160
PARIS TO SCOTLAND	173
SCOTLAND TO AMERICA	189
USEFUL HINTS FOR TRAVELLERS .	203

ILLUSTRATIONS.

	FACES PAGE
TWO VERMONT LADIES, *Frontispiece*	
FALLS OF TIVOLI	23
PLOUGHING IN EGYPT	29
HASHAM, OUR DRAGOMAN	33
DRAWING WATER ON THE NILE	39
SHEIK EL SADATH	62
WATER BOTTLES AND FILTERS OF EGYPT	64
SON OF A SHEIK	74
CROSSING THE JORDAN	78
THE JEWS' WAILING-PLACE	89
BEDOUINS WITH THEIR HARPS	103
VEILED WOMEN	109
ACROPOLIS AT ATHENS	139
TURKISH LADIES	153
MOSQUE OF THE SULTAN	158
ONE OF THE "BEEF-EATERS"	197

FROM VERMONT TO DAMASCUS.

The bleak, rugged winter of 1895 in Vermont, when Jack Frost held nightly carnivals and mercury was found in the lower regions, the snow was scurrying from hill-top to vale to find a resting place,— such environments caused the author of this little volume to dream of fairer skies and warmer climes. Sunny Italy, with her groves of orange and lemon trees, her gardens filled with fruit, her gladioli and lilies leading the flowery kingdom, was a drawing card to a Vermonter in the short days of January. Such a picture caused me to decide to leave old Vermont for the winter, spending my days farther south, until she had put on her summer garments, when she would become the loveliest spot on earth. About this time the clarion trumpet of Dr. A. E. Dunning, of the *Congregationalist*, was heard through the land, calling for fair women and brave men to join him in his Oriental tour. His itinerary through Italy, Egypt, and the Holy Land was an attractive one; and the die in my case was soon cast. Believing it to be an unwise thing for a married man to take such a journey without his wife, wisdom had its way. The party was made up from eleven different States. Miss Daniels, a charming young lady from Grafton, and the two members from Springfield, were the only representatives from Vermont. The number of our party to leave New York was, like Paul's chastisements, forty save one; and they were to be under the guiding care of "Henry Gaze & Sons," of London. The first essential step was to procure tickets, passports, letters of credit, suitable clothing, pluck, courage, and a determination to have a good time.

February 14th found us on board an express train, wending our way down the Connecticut Valley, stopping for a night at Hartford with friends, and reaching New York the 15th. That afternoon we attended a reception at the St. Denis Hotel, given by Dr. Dunning, where we were to meet those of the Oriental party that we had never met before, but were hoping for pleasant friendships with in the future.

Introductions, hand-shaking, coffee, and viands were the order of the afternoon; and every one seemed pleased with the other fellow, and the verdict was that the doctor had shown wisdom in making up his party for the Holy Land.

February 16th found us on board the "Normannia," and baggage nicely stowed away. Many friends of the Oriental party were on board with good wishes for a successful journey. Occasionally we saw a tear, but smiles predominated.

At twelve o'clock the whistle blew for all those not intending to sail to leave the boat. The gangplank was drawn in; and the "Normannia" weighed anchor, slowly swung her prow down the North River, and a journey of some eighteen thousand miles began.

ON THE WAY TO NAPLES.

My friends in Springfield who have never been down to the sea, or crossed the big waters, perhaps have but little idea of the skippers that take people across from the New to the Old World and *vice versa*. To give you the length in feet of the "Normannia" would convey but little; but, when I refer you to the Adnabrown Hotel, which is a long building of one hundred and fifty feet, and tell you to place three of them in line, and then add seventy feet, you would have the length of our beautiful steamer. It is two stories high besides the attic, with a cellar two stories deep, and is a regular floating palace. Few hotels in the country are fitted up as nicely. Her engines have sixteen thousand horse-power, several times the power of all the motor wheels in Black River at Springfield. She has nine boilers; and, when they run her full speed, it takes three hundred tons of coal every twenty-four hours.

Mr. and Mrs. Weeden met us at the boat when we left New York, and presented us with some beautiful flowers. It did us as much good as medicine to meet our old pastor and wife. Mr. Weeden is the personification of a true gentleman.

Our party are all together in the dining-room, occupying four tables, ten at each, save one seat which is occupied by the steamer physician, dressed in uniform. We have on board a fine German band that gives us a large quantity of splendid music.

We sailed Saturday, the 16th. Sunday we had religious services. Dr. Horton, of Providence, preached a ringing sermon from Exodus xxxiii. 13. At this writing we have been on the way one week, have encountered no gales, but have found the ocean rather rough, and have had many sick. Racks have been on the tables most of the time. Mrs. Brown and myself have been in the dining-room and on deck every day. Our captain is polite. He found out that he had some sight-seers on board. So he proposed to change his course a little, and take us through the Azores, which was quite a treat. We could, with our field-glasses, see the houses, and fields on the sides of the mountains. These islands are very high, some of them running up seven thousand feet. They belong to Portugal, and are inhabited by that race; and the islands are said to be large enough to support three hundred thousand people. They raise olives, oranges, pineapples, figs, etc. The pineapples, which are of a very superior quality, are raised under glass. The inside is free from any woody substance and so soft it can be eaten with a spoon. They command high prices, selling for three or four dollars each. London epicures fill them with wine, and consider them a great luxury. The government sends ships to them about once in two months, to receive and deliver mail and supplies. Mists and fogs from the ocean keep everything verdant.

Our ship "Normannia" is officered and manned entirely by Germans. They are very polite and attentive. The table is luxurious, from four to six courses, abundance of fruit, apples, pears, oranges, pineapples, grapes, bananas, etc. But the poet sings, "What is home without a mother?" So many of the passengers sing here, "What is dinner without an appetite?"

SATURDAY MORNING, 23d.

Had a smooth run last night, but have just met a north-easter this morning; and it looks as though we shall be "rocked in the cradle of the deep" for the next few hours. We expect to reach Gibraltar tomorrow night, where this letter will be sent ashore to take the first steamer for New York. We shall reach Naples Wednesday or Thursday, where I shall hope to write you again, as we expect to spend several days looking over the beautiful Bay of Naples, and get our feet on "terra cotta" again, as the man said, which we shall no doubt enjoy.

Sunday morning, instead of one of the band giving the trumpet call to rise, the whole band played a beautiful church hymn. It was very pleasant, and showed their respect for the day.

Just after the mail was closed on board the "Normannia," last Sunday, February 24, and my first letter to you was ready to start back for New York, we were beginning to sail up into the Straits of Gibraltar. It was a beautiful day, clear and balmy, mercury about seventy degrees. We had already sighted land on both sides of the channel; and, if you will take a seat with me on the upper deck, I will show you one of the finest pictures anywhere to be found,—the water smooth as glass, and the "Normannia" gliding through the water proudly as a queen. On our right you will see the coast of Africa, with rugged hills extending back, to all appearances, into the interior. On our left is the coast of Spain, with less rugged appearance, and I should say the much more desirable place for a habitation. We continue to narrow the channel until we reach the stone battlements. Some two miles before we reach this point, at our left, you will see the village of Trafalgar, where the great naval battle was fought and where Nelson lost his life. The town has the appearance of containing some fifteen hundred inhabitants, with buildings painted white, having a very neat appearance. The land for a mile or more up the channel has a very peculiar appearance, looking like the waves of the ocean laid up at an angle of fifteen degrees. With our glass we could see the beautiful green fields, divided into lots, with green hedge fences. All the time you are drinking in this beautiful picture the grand background will be the stone battlements of Gibraltar, just ahead of you, extending out into the channel. We reached this point just at sunset, which added greatly to the beauty of the picture. Just before reaching the fort, our steamer turns to the left into a beautiful bay or harbor, where we find war vessels of different nations. Saw the stars and stripes. The war-ship "Chicago" was anchored there. The Americans on board the "Normannia" cheered them with waving of pocket handkerchiefs. They returned it, and their band played one of our national airs. At this point we anchored; and small boats came out, and took mail, telegrams, passengers, etc. Many of our party went ashore, where you find Moors, Turks, and Spaniards, besides the soldiers. Selling rum and tobacco is the main business, and this is considered a wicked town. The streets are narrow and not lighted, houses built of stone several stories high. Back of the town is a wood where live the only wild monkeys known in Europe. It is a species *without tails* and one protected by the government. Whether this is because of the lack of this appendage I did not learn, but it no doubt had something to do with the matter.

Now, as you stand back down the channel, Gibraltar looks like a big Dutchman with a cap on, standing as sentinel, guarding the traffic from ocean to the sea. It rises fourteen hundred feet above the sea, is seven miles in circumference, and is connected with the mainland by a narrow strip of flat ground. It is composed largely of limestone, some marble, and was naturally full of caverns and cavities. In addition to this, England has honeycombed it through and through; and no one but the British war department and the soldiers know what there is inside. There are five thousand soldiers quartered here, and one thousand cannon. England spends a million a year running this Dutchman.

It was about 1785 when Spain and France combined to take this fortress away from England, and had a three years' siege, but had to give it up. It is said to be the strongest and most important fort in the world. At six o'clock there was a cannon fired.

This was a signal for every stranger to go outside the walls unless he had a permit from the head officer.

I will give you the outlines of one of the big guns at Gibraltar. Length, thirty-two feet; size of bore, 17.72 inches; the charge is five feet long; weight of powder, four hundred fifty pounds; weight of ball, two thousand pounds; force of blow, thirty-three thousand tons; distance, eight miles; will pierce twenty-five inches solid iron. This gun is fired only on the queen's birthday and special occasions, at which time notice is given, and windows are raised in all the buildings to prevent the breaking of glass.

The "Normannia" left Gibraltar 7.30 Sunday eve. We had a smooth sail, and slept finely, quite different from what we found it on the old Atlantic.

MONDAY MORNING.

We are sailing up the Mediterranean, which is lovely; and every one seems to be gathering up from the rough voyage of last week. We reached Algiers about 7 P.M., sailing up past Morocco. Algiers has about sixty thousand people, is controlled by the French. About sixteen thousand of that nationality were taken by the French in 1830. They have a large Arab settlement. Then there are Moors, Jews, Buddhists, etc., etc. As I said, the "Normannia" reached Algiers at seven in the evening, and was to leave at eleven. The town rises from the coast very abruptly, is lighted with gas, and looks fine from the boat. Having three hours to ourselves, we took small boats that the natives were running in the bay, and went ashore, then took carriages, and drove through the town two hours, driving through the Arab district. We saw Oriental life in full bloom; and from what we saw of the natives we soon made up our minds they were a people we should not care to sleep with, and were careful to be back on the "Normannia" before the hour of her departure.

Tuesday morning, bright and clear, and we are still sailing up the Mediterranean, water smooth as a glassy lake, the air soft and balmy, every one happy. Expect to reach Naples to-morrow at eleven.

The "Normannia," which showed her antics on the old ocean, striking her nose into those big, rolling waves, throwing the water over her deck and bows, sending it rushing down by our cabin windows, seemed to have sown her wild oats before she reached Gibraltar, and has given us a splendid sail through the Mediterranean. We think of our Springfield friends, and wish we could treat them to a day's sail on this beautiful sea, and enjoy the balmy air of a Vermont June day.

LETTERS FROM ITALY.

I.

NAPLES, Feb. 27, 1895.

We arrived at this place to-day at eleven o'clock A.M., at which time you were, no doubt, rubbing your eyes, and deciding whether you would turn out for a day's work or have another nap before doing so, as we have gained six hours since leaving New York, and shall probably, for the present, leave Springfield time in the shade.

As we sailed up the Bay of Naples, we saw in our front a beautiful city of some three hundred thousand people. The city was in amphitheatre style, lying in the form of a crescent, buildings largely white, from one to six stories high, nestling among the palms, olives, figs, lemons, orange, and pine trees, and a great variety of tropical plants, giving a beautiful contrast. This, encircling the bay, gave us a picture of rare beauty. The "Normannia" anchored in the bay, and small steamers came and took the passengers and baggage ashore. Seemingly one-half on board left the steamer at this place. The custom-house officers here are very strict, but the Gaze Company had made arrangements to let us through without a very rigid examination. Cigars, tobacco, and liquors are what they are after; and our crowd were pretty well played out in those goods before we reached Naples. Nine cigars, or what they call a day's stock, is all a man can bring ashore without duty. Naples has impressed me as a charming place. It is, in my opinion, the "Pasadena" of this section of country. Some Americans may desire to be wedded to this charming spot, but I am willing to admire its beauty and pass on. America is good enough for me. The customs are exceedingly funny here, and no doubt will appear so all our journey through. Everything in the way of traffic moves slowly, and is queerly done. You will see an ox and a cow yoked together, next a cow and a horse; and then will come along a horse, cow, and donkey, all attached to the same vehicle. The little donkeys that are driven in the two-wheel carts would set young America in Springfield wild. As to horses, they go from the ridiculous to the sublime, from the poor creatures to turnouts that will match anything in Saratoga. They seem to vie with each other in trimming and ornamenting their harness, tugs, breeching, bridles; and every conceivable strap is filled with brass or nickel nails, studs, or buckles. The driving of the pleasure teams is like Jehu,— furiously.

The great nuisance of the country is beggars, hucksters, and hawkers. The beggars will beset you while walking or riding. They will run beside your carriage with an alertness that indicates training in the business.

The arrangement for delivering milk will, no doubt, interest our milkmen in Vermont. The cows are driven into the city twice a day. You will see a man with one or more. A woman will come out with a tumbler, the man milks it full, and she pays him two cents for it. He then drives on, furnishing his customers with any quantity desired. Goat's milk is furnished in the same way. You will see droves of from ten to forty of them. This milk, they claim, is for the children; and there is no end to their number. The woods are full of children here in Naples. These goats are driven mostly on the sidewalks, and have equal rights with the pedestrians. The teams and traffic go on in the streets. However, they have one advantage over us: they need no law against the adulteration of milk.

As I said at the commencement of this letter, we reached this place on Wednesday, the 27th, about noon; and, as we had been on the "Normannia" eleven days, we took our lunch, and then spent the rest of the afternoon in resting, looking among the stores, getting our bearings, etc. Thursday at 8.30 our carriages were ready, our managers on hand with all their plans made, and we took a drive through the city, in the forenoon going through the museum, said to be one of the most wonderful in the world; that is, for antiquity. Here we found the relics from Pompeii, showing plainly there were art and science in those days. One thing that impressed me was a hot-water heater for warming their rooms, also instruments for examining the stomach. I told Dr. Dunning we ought to have had one on the steamer during the rough days on the ocean. Of ancient glass, statuary, etc., there was no end. The kings and queens of ancient days were there. Our managers through their efforts had secured a chance for us to visit the royal palace. This was a treat of a lifetime. So, after leaving the museum, we went directly there. We first went to the gardens on top of buildings, then we descended and commenced the apartments, and I should say we went through some thirty of them, — the theatre, banquet-room, chapel, banquet hall, common dining-room, office, study of the king, throne-room, etc. Such splendor I had never imagined before. The wall and ceiling were covered with the richest of Gobelin tapestry, the finish and furniture of blue and gold, and white and gold. Our eyes were dazzled more than I expect they will be with the rays of the Egyptian sun. From this place we returned to our Hotel Royal, and had lunch. Then we took our carriages again, and drove through the orange and lemon groves, some eight miles, to Puteoli, where Saint Paul landed on his way to Rome as a prisoner. (See Acts xxviii. 13.) From this place he struck The Three Taverns, where his friends met him, and Paul thanked God, and took courage. We expect to go to Rome to-morrow. Whether we shall stop at The Three Taverns or not, I cannot say to-day, but may write you later. On the way out to Puteoli we visited the tomb of Virgil. Had a full and delightful day. Friday morning we took a small steamer, and had one and a half hour's sail across the Bay of Naples to Sorrento. Sailed along near the base of Mt. Vesuvius, and could almost hear the boiling and hissing of the elements within. The smoke and flames can be plainly seen from our hotel. We reached Sorrento before lunchtime. Stopped at Hotel Victoria, which is designed for tourists and is beautiful in all its arrangements, standing upon a high cliff of perpendicular lime-rock. You can stand on the front court and drop a pebble two hundred feet into the Mediterranean Sea. Sorrento is said to be the Mecca for tourists. You have the blue waters of the Mediterranean in front of you, and the mountains wild, yet cultivated and beautiful, behind you. They are made up of ravines and ridges, terraced and fruit-bearing to the top, where you see the vineyards. Added to that are the lemon, orange, and figs, with a large abundance of olives, the peculiar color of the olive leaf giving the landscape a soft, velvety appearance which is very pleasing to the eye. The roads that have been built by the government around and about and over these mountains are just wonderful. They are macadamized with the limestone, which is broken up by hand by the natives. On the sides heavy stone-faced walls beautifully laid, it must be by skilled hands. After lunch we took a ride on one of these roads to the top of the mountain, visiting an institution called "La Deserta," home for orphan children. The managers were glad to see us, treated us with their native wine and oranges. From the top of this building we had one of the grandest views that often fall to the lot of man to revel in. From this point we returned to our hotel.

After dinner we were invited to an entertainment arranged by our managers. This was given in a hall in our hotel by some twenty Italians, mostly young people, instrumental and vocal music, with acting and dancing which was modestly and beautifully done ; and much of it was original and very amusing. Some of our ministers laughed more that evening than they have before for twelve months. All I could say was, " Well done, boys and girls of Italy."

Saturday morning we took carriages for Pompeii. This ride of sixteen miles is said to be the second finest in all Europe. We had the beautiful blue waters of the sea on one hand and the towering mountains, ravines, and ridges with the tropical verdure on the other, and a road so fine that horses did not break the trot the whole distance. At Pompeii we had lunch, then spent two hours with guides travelling through the ruins of that wonderful city. They are still excavating, had just uncovered a beautiful mansion with fine statuary, paintings, etc. This was interesting to us, as most of the furnishings and fittings have been carried away. We saw many of them in the museum at Naples. They send officers with you, and do not allow you to take away the first particle of anything; but I imagine a little dust stuck to some of our party before they left the city.

Some of the party went up Mount Vesuvius, and returned to Naples by train in the evening. The others took carriages for Naples, reaching there at 5 P.M.

A quiet Sunday has been spent here, some attending church. To-morrow morning at 7.30 we expect to start for Rome, reaching there about noon, leaving there for this place again. Saturday we leave here for Brindisi, where we take steamer for Egypt.

II.

ROME, March 4, 1895.

You will remember that in my last letter I left you at Naples. After that time we visited the old aqueduct, built through the mountain by Nero, to bring the water into Naples. When we were on our way from Pompeii, we saw parts of the old Appian Way, built by Nero from Naples to Rome, over which Saint Paul travelled on his way from Puteoli to Rome, when a prisoner. All roads lead to Rome, and this was one of them.

We took an early start this morning, left our hotel at 7 A.M. and took train for this place. Our managers had secured two cars for us, so we were not obliged to mix up with the natives. These cars will be held here at Rome until Friday, when we shall return to Naples. Saturday the same cars will take us to Brindisi, where we take steamer for Egypt. This was our first car-ride in the old country, and we were interested to know the result, as they tell great stories about their fast trains, etc. One of their yarns is that a young man was on one of their fast express trains, and was going through a town where his lady love resided : he wired her to be on the platform of the station, as he wished to kiss her as he passed through. She was there ; but the train went so fast that, instead of kissing his lady love, he kissed a peasant at the next station. Bad egg. Now do not be anxious about us : there is no flirtation in our company. However, we found the train a very good one, and made the one hundred and sixty miles in five hours; but we think Uncle Sam is ahead yet on speed and quality of service.

Starting out from Naples, we found the finest farming lands that ever mortals set eyes upon. Judge Whitmore, of Pennsylvania, who is one of our party, and has travelled extensively, said he never saw the like before. The land was a level plain, and rich in the extreme. There were a great many olive, mulberry and fig trees scattered over it; but under, through, and among them the ground was covered with vegetation, and for some ten miles out it was largely garden vegetables. It was like riding through a grove and garden combined. Everything here is done by hand, and largely the old bog hoe, as we call it, is used, — this, with a round stick driven in for a handle. Occasionally we would see men working with long-handled spades or shovels, which looked quite modern. As we speed on our way, this broad plain begins to narrow in upon us, and the foothills were at one time down near the track; but every foot of ground in this country seems to be cultivated, even to the tops of the mountains. Before we reached Rome, this valley we had been passing over began to widen; and, when we caught sight of the ancient city, it appeared to be standing at the head of a broad plain. As we neared the city, we saw the old stone aqueducts resting upon hundreds of stone arches. When our train drew into the depot, we were surprised to find a building of modern structure; and, as we came outside, we learned the fact that we were in what is called New Rome, which has a very modern appearance. Carriages soon took us to the Hotel d'Angleterre, which is very satisfactory.

After lunch our managers took us to the Pincian Hill, and gave us a bird's-eye view of Rome, pointing out the places of interest that we should visit between this time and Friday. At the foot of this hill is a park where stands Cleopatra's Needle. At your right is the old gate to the city where the pilgrims entered. Here Martin Luther entered, and at your left stands the church where he took his first communion. A little farther in front flows the river Tiber, with its large number of bridges spanning its waters, and its splendid stone masonry up and down its banks as far as you can see. Beyond this river stands St. Peter's Church, with its sixteen domes, the main dome being some four hundred feet high, length of church six hundred feet, width four hundred and fifty feet; and at the right of this wonderful structure stands the Vatican, where resides the pope. After we had our fill of gazing over the city, we descended to the foot of the hill, where we took carriages, and drove to St. Peter's Church. First you enter the square in front, containing some acres. At your right and left begin the circling colonnades. Upon the top of these, which extend up to the church, stand statues of the saints, some two hundred of them.

As you go up the long line of stone steps and enter the church, your first impression is its immensity. As you go on, this feeling grows upon you; and you are awed with its grandeur. Outside it has a dingy appearance; but a great amount of money is expended inside to keep it in fine condition, and it attracts the eye of all lovers of the beautiful. Our manager explained everything as we went through this great building, which took nearly one hour. This church was nearly three hundred years in building, and was begun in the fourteenth century. We went down into the vault, and they unlocked the door and showed us the box that held, as they claim, the ashes of Saint Peter. The leaving of this church closed quite an eventful day for us; and we went to our hotel for dinner and a good night's rest, which brought us out all right.

Tuesday morning at nine o'clock we took carriages, and drove to the Pantheon. This is a building of historical interest. It was built twenty-seven years before Christ by Marcus Agrippa. First he intended it for the people as a public bathing-place. It was the first brick building ever erected, also the first dome architecture. One immense dome covers the whole building. It pleased the people and its builder so much that in dedicating it any individual god was not sufficient, and so it was dedicated to the gods, which gave it the name Pantheon. It is now used as a church, and services were going on while we were looking it over. From this building we drove to the Vatican. This building contains eleven hundred rooms. Of course, we did not try to take in the whole thing, but spent some two hours inside; and I will mention only a few things that impressed me most. One was the pope's private chapel, which no one visits without permission. The decoration was done by Michel Angelo; and at one end of this chapel is his masterpiece, called "The Judgment," upon which he nearly lost his eyesight. In going through the museum of this building, you will make up your mind that marble, onyx, talent, and time have made obeisance to the pope. From all parts of Italy and Greece have been gathered the finest of everything. When you enter the rotunda, you will notice a gilt bronze statue of Hercules, some twelve feet high, standing with a lion skin thrown over one arm, the other hand holding an immense club resting on the ground. Fabulous sums of money have been offered for this statue, but it cannot be bought. It is said that the Vatican and what is in it cost more than all the wealth of Italy. St. Peter's Church is said to have cost twelve million pounds sterling, and at that time that sum meant much more than it does now. We have visited the building where the apostles were thrust into the inner prison, and I can say that I never had much of an idea before of that place. We took candles, and went down into a dungeon. Then they told us that the inner prison was under that. So on down we went; and, if the word dismal has any significance, we found it there, stone above, below, and around you. We visited the spot where once stood the monument inscribed " to the unknown god." The emperor at that time was warned, as he claimed, by some god that the enemy was approaching, and went and conquered them. Not knowing the god that did him this favor, he had the statue or monument erected and thus inscribed. We visited the Palatine Hill where once stood Cæsar's palace. Everything on this hill, you doubtless know, was destroyed by the Gauls and Vandals, being burned and pulled down; and, as other kings have built their palaces in other parts of the city, they have taken everything of value, and it looks now like the ruins of an immense castle. The government is at work excavating and clearing up matters; but the subterranean caverns, arches, etc., that the palace stood upon are wonderful. We stood on the spot where Paul stood when he appealed to Cæsar for justice, and the foundation of the throne where Cæsar sat is still intact. At the base of the Palatine Hill stand the three pillars of Castor and Pollux, near the Forum. These pillars were once greatly admired for their symmetrical beauty. Pliny tells us of a raven that was hatched upon the roof of the Temple of Castor and Pollux, that flew into a bootmaker's shop opposite. Every morning it used to fly to the Rostra which looked toward the Forum, where he would salute the Emperor Tiberius and others as they passed by, after which he returned to the shop, doing this for several years and being a great pet. But through the jealousy of an owner of an opposition shop the bird was killed, and for this the man was put to death. The bird had a public funeral, with a larger concourse of people than ever attended any king.

The old historical interest of Rome would fill volumes. I am drinking in what I can of it, and will give you a few more items of this ancient city in my next letter.

III.

ROME, March 8, 1895.

Still in sunny Italy. For the last few days we have been busy looking over the interesting parts of the city, but will not trouble you with detail in the matter, but would like to give you a general idea of Rome. Romulus pitched his tent here seven hundred and fifty years before the Christian era, and in the nearly three thousand years Rome has had a wonderful experience. At times she ruled the world, then again without prestige. Century after century has crumbled into dust, and the people of to-day are walking over their ashes. The martyrdom of the apostles was at their hand. They slaughtered the Christians, and scattered them to the four corners of the earth; but their cup has been a bitter one, and they have drained it to the dregs. But the stone that was cut out of the mountain has triumphed, and the sun of righteousness is reflecting its light back upon its persecutors; and Rome is to-day rising in her Christian civilization. If you will take a ramble with me, I will show you a city pretty free from saloons and drunkenness, streets beautifully paved and kept remarkably clean; a city with fine hotels, stores full of fine goods, merchants polite, many of the clerks speak English, pure water in abundance; and no city with so great number of fountains, many of them not excelled in beauty in any city. Then look for a moment upon her historical interest, her massive walls that surrounded the city with her many watchtowers and battlement, its gates bolted and barred,

FALLS OF TIVOLI.

but now a thing of the past, her ruined temples and palaces, her old stone aqueduct that has given way to the modern iron pipe. These things are drawing tourists, English as well as American. The Methodists are building a fine mission building here, which is soon to be dedicated. Many from America are expected at the dedication. We are glad this town was in our route, and shall leave it with regrets. Our stay here has been full of interest.

Our party this morning took a carriage for a depot on the east side of the city, and took train for Tivoli. Crossing the large plain we came over on our arrival, eighteen miles brought us to the foot of the Sabine Hills. Up this elevation our train went, wending its way through thousands of acres of olive-trees, until it had carried us some five hundred feet above the level of the plain, and landed us in Tivoli. This town is many years older than Rome. West, some twenty miles distant, you see Rome with the dome of St. Peter's Church. Tivoli is about half-way up the Sabine Hills. Back of this elevation are the Apennines, whence comes a great quantity of pure spring water. The Sabine Hills are composed of lime-rock; and the water from the Apennines comes through caverns under the town, and makes its appearance in different places one side of the town, and tumbles down three hundred feet into a ravine. The water, running continually, is twice as much as runs in Black River, at Springfield, when it is at its usual height. Walks have been built up and down these cascades. The beautiful rainbow is there when the sun shines, and it is a grand sight to behold.

Here is a great electric plant that furnishes the lights for Rome : here, also, Rome takes its water supply. After looking over these beautiful falls and the old town and taking our lunch, we took teams and drove to the plains, and visited the wonderful ruins of Hadrian's castle, or palace. Hadrian ruled Rome — in fact, the world — twenty-one years in the first part of the second century. He did much to fortify different places, and at the same time spent fabulous sums for himself, and has left the largest ruins probably known. His palace was a mile long, everything conceivable connected with it. We found in the flooring some of the finest mosaic work known. Bathing-houses, swimming and rowing, sports and games of all kinds, were, no doubt, carried on there.

While here at Tivoli, we saw them ploughing with several yoke of oxen. The ploughs were wooden beams, with a wooden prong running down into the ground, and one piece of wood coming up for a handle. Whether these were the same oxen that Elisha was ploughing with when the Lord called upon him I am not prepared to say; but the oxen here are very peculiar-looking, with immense horns running up into the air, and look like the pictures of the sacred cattle. Almost all of them are white. You will see large flocks of sheep corralled at night, led out by the shepherds daytimes.

We left Rome Friday morning, had a very pleasant trip to Naples, where we were to spend the night. On our arrival we found there had been an Austrian steamer run on the rocks in the Bay of Naples, and four hundred passengers taken off and put into the hotel. So our managers could not get rooms satisfactory to them, and put us on a train and took us some fifteen miles, to Castellamare, to a fine hotel, where we had excellent quarters for the night. Saturday, March 9, we took train for Brindisi, two hundred and sixty miles distant. This gave us another view of Italy, crossing over sections of the Apennines. We had quite a long train with three engines going up the mountains, two in front and one in the rear. It was a miniature picture of our trip over the Rocky Mountains on our way from California. That was ten thousand feet above the sea. This was four thousand, but the ragged cliffs and the forty tunnels we passed through had the appearance of the Rockies with their snowsheds. These tunnels were from one hundred feet to a mile in length: the snow covered the ground on this elevation. After passing over these mountains, we dropped down into a luxuriant valley in Eastern Italy. Trains here run no dining-cars, and very slight accommodations in the depots for feeding people. So our managers had lunch put up for us at the hotel where we stayed the night before; and we had a jolly time with a picnic dinner, and reached Brindisi at 7 P.M., where we had a full dinner at the hotel. Our steamer, which is a very large one, nearly as large as the " Normannia," lay waiting for us in front of the hotel. We went aboard about ten. The next day, March 10, we were on the Mediterranean, which at this time is smooth and glassy.

IV.

MONDAY, the 11th.

We came on deck this morning and found that we were sailing under the island of Crete; but you will remember that in the Epistle to Titus Paul did not give the natives a very good reputation. So we decided not to call on them, but shall push on to Alexandria, which place we expect to reach to-morrow night or Wednesday morning. The captain tells us that we are running ahead of time. The sea is calm and beautiful. We saw it last evening by moonlight, which was a picture of a lifetime. Our party are all well and we are congratulating ourselves in being so fortunate in having so smooth a sea for our four days' sail over these waters that are liable to be turbulent.

In looking over the working classes of Italy, we find men and women both work as farm hands. The men receive from thirty to forty cents per day, the women from fifteen to twenty; and they board themselves. The tax paid to the government is enormous.

LETTERS FROM EGYPT.

I.

MARCH 13, 1895.

We reached Alexandria several hours ahead of time, and were landed safely. You may be interested in knowing more fully the method of taking on and off passengers and baggage from the large steamers that we have been travelling on. Occasionally they have a chance to land at a wharf, but usually they anchor out in the bay; and small boats come from the shore, and take from the steamer all that wish to land. When the steamer is anchored, and gives the signal that everything is ready, there starts from the shore anywhere from ten to forty Arabs, Turks, Moors, etc., with turbans on their heads, clad in either gowns or Turkish trousers, bare feet and legs, in their little boats, talking and shouting at the top of their voices, rowing for dear life; for the first one to the steamer expects to get his boat full. Being in an unknown tongue, it is a perfect pandemonium. Up they come, climbing up the side of the vessel like a pack of pirates; but, as our managers have the entire charge of our transportation, we have nothing to do but stand back and enjoy the fracas. This small boat arrangement is all right with a smooth sea, but with a rough surf it means business. The laws of different cities usually regulate the price these boatmen should charge; but, when they get hold of Americans that are not posted, they will fleece them every time.

The "Thalia," that brought us from Brindisi to Alexandria, nearly one thousand miles, is a boat nearly four hundred feet long, manned by Austrians. They gave us good service, and were polite and attentive. When we took carriages for our hotel, a foreign country dawned upon us as never before. Camels with solemn tread, bearing heavy burdens, the streets full of donkeys, the people with their turbans, gowns, and Turkish trousers, women with the water-bottles on their heads, blacksmiths with their anvils on the sidewalk in front of their shops, hammering iron, the shoemakers and other mechanics in the same way, having their shops, but working in front in the open air. The Turkish gown and trousers is the common garb. The police here, as well as in Naples and Rome, carry the sword instead of the billy, and here in Alexandria most of them are mounted on fine horses. Everywhere they are in uniform.

After lunch we took carriages, and drove most of the afternoon. Went out and visited Pompey's Pillar, which is a wonderful monument of granite. The base is about fifteen feet square, ten feet high; and then there is a round, solid shaft, made out of one stone, about nine feet in diameter, seventy feet high, with a capstone that would weigh, in my opinion, ten tons. How this pillar was set up on end, and that capstone placed in position, is a mystery to the mechanic of the nineteenth century. This was erected in honor of Pompey, after his death. He

PLOUGHING IN EGYPT.

was beloved by the people, as he had fed them many times in famine. From this point we went to a villa and beautiful garden owned by one Antonides, a Greek merchant. These grounds are said to be the finest in Egypt. The khedive's palace we could not get a permit to enter. Our drive ended about 6 P.M., landing us at our Hotel Abbas, where we were soon ready for dinner, and spent a restful night.

The next morning we took train for Cairo, one hundred and thirty miles, and made the run in three and a half hours. The country through which we came was perfectly level, lying but a little above the level of the sea. Most of the way we followed the canal that was cut through years ago from Cairo to Alexandria, connecting the Nile with that place and the sea, through which a great amount of traffic passes, not drawn by horses, as in America, but with sail and row boats. Our ride from Alexandria took us through a rich farming country, which seemed to be covered with crops. The work here is done differently from what it is in Italy. Instead of the hand work, the soil is lightened up with the old wooden plough drawn by oxen. The Egyptian cattle are peculiar looking, coarse, large size, with horns growing directly backward, close to the neck. Oxen and cows are both used to draw the wooden plough. Everything about their work is of the crudest character. The yoke is a round stick some four inches in diameter, perfectly straight, and about eight feet long, lying upon the neck with ropes instead of bows to hold it on. I have had a curiosity to examine one of these ploughs. I went for an old fellow to-day that I saw ploughing in a field, but, when I reached him, could not make him understand what I wanted. So I caught hold of his plough, and pulled it out of the ground. There was no mould-board to turn over the soil, but they do have a piece of iron on the point. This drawn through the ground has a tendency to lighten it up. The soil is rich and lumpy; and on the Nile they use only sand brought from the desert to improve their crops, which are wheat, barley, flax, onions, cucumbers, etc. Egypt raises immense quantities of onions. We have not seen as yet many orange groves; but there are sections where they are produced in abundance, as we can find all we want, large, sweet, and juicy, for one cent apiece. There is no tobacco raised in Egypt. If a man should have a piece of ground two feet square covered with tobacco, he would be liable to imprisonment for ten years. Great quantities are brought in from other countries, with a heavy duty. This gives the government a large revenue, and is the reason why the people are not allowed to raise it. The people here are ground to the earth by taxation. American slavery, that we used to have, would be far preferable. Wages here are ten cents a day, and the laborer boards himself. Every palm-tree is taxed, and everything that a man raises. Every village has its sheik, or what we might call one of the khedive's lieutenants, and rules with an iron hand; and, if a man cannot pay his tax, he is bastinadoed until his cries excite the sympathy of his friends, and they come and pay the amount required.

As we left Alexandria, we first saw the Arab villages built of dried mud, — anywhere from twenty to a hundred of these mud boxes, clustered together, with alley-ways between them. Some were thatched on top with straw, others had a dome top built with mud. Here men, women, and children, goats, chickens, and donkeys, find a home. All seemingly are living together. Here by these villages they bury their dead, graves or tombs being above ground, built of same material as their houses. Many of these burying structures are whitewashed.

Our first plans were to spend several days in Cairo before going up the Nile; but on our arrival it was thought best to start up the Nile at once, and visit Cairo on our return, which will be the first week in April. This letter will be mailed at Rhodes. My next letter will be the commencing of the Nile tour.

II.

ON THE NILE, March 17, 1895.

My last letter was written when we first commenced our trip up this wonderful river, but it was about matters that my eye had witnessed before reaching Cairo. On our arrival at Cairo, which was Wednesday, the 13th, about noon, carriages took us direct to the "Memphis," our Nile boat, which was to start up the river at 5 P.M. This boat was chartered by the Gaze Company expressly for our party, which just fills all the cabins on the boat. It is about one hundred and ninety feet long, considered one of the best on the river, and is more than satisfactory to our party.

After lunch we took carriages for two hours, and went to the stores, as many of the party wished to make purchases for the Nile tour, which it is expected will be a warm one, and needs a light headgear, white umbrella, etc. These are needed when we take our horseback or donkey rides from different landings out into the country, of which we have some ten.

The Nile is said to be the most wonderful river in the world, thirty-three hundred miles long. The last twelve hundred miles not a tributary enters it; and the amount of water it pours into the sea after its evaporation in travelling three thousand miles through the desert, and its countless irrigating canals in Egypt, transforming this section of country into the most fertile land in the world, make it wonderful. Egypt is often said to be the gift of the Nile, a mere strip of alluvial soil bordering the river on either side, from one-half to thirty miles wide. All the rest is a broad desert. The source has been and still is a mystery, though the late explorations make it possible that the great lake, Victoria Nyanza, is its feeder. The melting of the snow on the far-off mountains is the cause of its rise and overflow. But the historical associations are more interesting than its natural features. On its banks was developed the oldest civilization of the world. Its massive monuments along its banks are a matter of interest to-day. It had the honor of cradling the Deliverer of the nations. As we left Cairo, we were

HASHAM, OUR DRAGOMAN.

pointed out the spot where Pharaoh's daughter found Moses.

Our party are confident of an interesting time going up and down these great waters. They have boats here with cabins in the centre, enough for ten or twelve persons, with place in front end of boat for ten oarsmen, five on a side, with very long oars. The natives row finely, dipping their oars at exactly the same time, running their boats rapidly. These boats are chartered by parties going up and down the Nile. We met yesterday a gentleman and his family from California in one of them, coming down the river. Some of our party have the American flag with them. This was flung to the breeze as we passed them, and the cheers went back and forth in great earnest. We felt for a moment as though we were the other side of the Atlantic.

Well, to go back to the starting-point. Five o'clock Wednesday, the 13th, all on board, with our luggage packed away in our cabins, our steamer that was lying close to the Rasr el-Nil bridge, that is twelve hundred and sixty feet long, built by a French company, and is a model of work well done, started her engines, and swung out into the broad river, and our journey of twenty-one days on its smooth waters had begun. The Gaze Company have engaged a dragoman named Hasham, who was born in Arabia, but has been educated and lived in Egypt, to take this Nile trip with us. Hasham knows the country, and can handle the natives that we shall have much to do with in our short excursions we are to take from the boat.

At dinner, which was served at six, Hasham came in, and gave notice that breakfast would be at six to-morrow morning, rising bell would ring at five. Some of our ladies thought this was starting rather early; but as the first donkey ride was to commence then, I think they would have met the requirements if it had been three o'clock. But Thursday morning found every one on hand. Our boat had the evening before run up the river fifteen miles, and anchored at Bedrashayn; and, when we came out from breakfast, we saw on the bank of the river forty Arabs, each one with a donkey all saddled and bridled and ready for the fracas. The saddles and bridles are furnished by the Gaze Company, and are first-class. Soon we were all mounted and on our way. Every donkey was followed by an Arab, who was anxious to have his donkey get to the point of destination first, and would put it into the gallop, and run behind with the alertness of an antelope. One thing was wonderful,— among the forty people of our party there was not a poor rider: even the ladies were all fine riders. This excursion would have been a good entertainment for any New England village. Our first stop was at the sarcophagus of Rameses II., which was immense in size. We also went into his tomb. We also visited the ancient site of Memphis. This is supposed to be the oldest or first settlement in Egypt. It has been buried by the sand that has blown from the desert; but parts of it have been excavated, and interesting relics brought to light. We visited some of the Pyramids, also the tombs where the bones of the sacred bulls were buried. We were back again at our boat at eleven o'clock, having ridden fifteen miles. On our return came through an Arab village, saw misery in full bloom, looked into the school-rooms with children sitting on the ground, looked into the dark, smoky, dingy hovels where human beings stay, not live, but know nothing better, and were thankful that the lines had fallen to us in Christian America. We rode through fields of wheat, barley, flax, everything luxuriant; and, if a Christian civilization could be introduced, there would be no reason why these should not be the happiest people in the world.

At noon our boat started up the river, continuing its course until evening, then tying up for the night, which seems to be the custom of all boats on the Nile. This gave us a fine opportunity to sleep, making the trip delightful. Friday we were on the river all day, resting from our donkey ride the day before, having a chance to admire the scenery, which is constantly changing, with its groves of palms, fields of grain, villages, etc.

About 7 P.M. we reached Minieh, where we tied up for the night. This is a large place, with post and telegraph offices and the largest sugar factory in Egypt. Our dragoman, Mr. Hasham, proposed to have us visit these works, as they are running night and day. So with guides with lanterns we started through the town to the mill, and it proved very interesting to us. We had never seen anything of the kind before, commencing where the cane was taken from the wagons, put on tramways carrying it into the mill to the ponderous rolls where it was crushed, juice pressed out, which went into the tanks, the pulp going on to other tramways, carried out doors again, where it is dried and used for fuel. We followed the process of making the sugar, consisting of many different operations, until it came out granulated sugar, many of us taking samples that we will bring home. This mill employs two thousand men. The overseers get some $2.00 or $2.50 per day, but the bulk of them get from five to twenty cents per day. I have the impression the night and day help change at midnight, as there were hundreds lying about in the mill, asleep on the stone floor. Some had a piece of burlap under them, others the bare stone. The heat in the mill must have been ninety or one hundred degrees. The sugar is not as white as our granulated.

Early Saturday morning we reached Beni-Hassan, where we visited the tombs of Ameni and Knum hotep, calling for another donkey ride of about half the distance of the one we took Thursday. It is said there is the toughest set of Arabs here of any place on the river, and it was pathetic and amusing to see our dragoman Hasham lash them with his big cudgel of a whip he carried. He also provided two policemen with guns to go along with the party. But everything went off like clock-work; and it was the verdict of every one, Well done, Mr. Dragoman.

Saturday night we anchored in the river. About five Sunday morning the boat started, and ran up to Assiout, arriving about 7 A.M., where we tied up for the forenoon. This is a large town, some forty thousand, of whom twelve thousand are said to be Christians. Here the Presbyterians have a large mission station. We attended divine service. While everything was in an unknown tongue, yet it was interesting to see them. The audience consisted of about four hundred young men and boys and one hundred girls. They all sang with a will, and gave strict attention to the sermon, singing American tunes. One was "St. Martin." I could handle the tune.better than I could the words. To cater to the laws of the land, the girls sat by themselves in the front pews, with a curtain drawn across the church, not so high but what those behind could see the minister, who stood on a platform raised some three feet. The majority of the young men were fine-looking,— that is, fine features and form,— but dark skin. This work was commenced 1852, has been largely among the Coptics, though many Mohammedans have come in. The Coptics are what would be called a corrupt Christianity. This mission's headquarters are here; but they work all over Egypt, and have thousands in their churches. The work was very slow at first, but of late years has been making progress. Mr. Alexander, the minister, met us after meeting, and gave us a brief history of the work and the people.

Coming from church, we went through the business bazaars. Everything running in full bloom. Surely, Egypt is an Oriental country. You see it at every turn you make.

At 5 P.M. the Rev. Mr. Darsie, of Kentucky, who is one of our party, preached to us on deck. Dr. Dunning read the Scriptures, reading the story of Joseph's brethren going down to Egypt to buy corn. He said he took that subject because he should never have a chance to read it again on the ground where the scene transpired and his audience would never hear it again under existing circumstances. Our clergyman claims that Pharaoh lived very near Cairo, either Memphis, the ruins that we visited at the commencement of the journey, or Yoan, which is a little nearer Cairo than Memphis.

MONDAY MORNING.

We had a warm night. Mercury this morning stands at seventy.

We are now passing quite a large town. The banks are lined with Arabs, boat-loads of stone water-bottles going down the river.

III.

LUXOR ON THE NILE, March 20, 1895.

I will commence my sixth letter at this place. Have been one week with the prow of our boat pointing toward the source of this great river. Another week, and we shall begin to think of right about face, and follow the current down to Cairo from whence we started. We are enjoying the water, and the eleven thousand miles of water travel we shall have before we reach Springfield ought to make us pretty good sailors. Coming up the river, we have, with other things, been watching the methods of irrigation. The more ancient and crude way is a flaring

DRAWING WATER ON THE NILE.

vessel that will hold one or two pailfuls, with two ropes some eight feet long fastened one on each side. Two men, one at the end of each rope, will swing the vessel into the river in a way that it fills, then, throwing it upon the bank striking bottom side up, emptying the water into the sluice-ways, where it runs off into their gardens and fields. The rapidity with which these men will throw this vessel and the quantity of water that will run from one of them are surprising. This works where the bank is only some five feet high or less. Another arrangement is an old-fashioned well-sweep. This will take the water up high embankments, as the first man draws it, say eight feet, and pours it into a shallow well dug in the bank. From this the next man takes it, and so on to the top, where it is carried in trenches as before. The third and better way is two wheels, one horizontal, the other perpendicular. The latter has an endless chain running over it, long enough to go down into the water. On this chain are hanging buckets that are coming up full of water, emptying at the top into a trough, and going on down empty. The other wheel that carries this has an ox or horse or some animal attached to it, and goes round like the horse grinding mortar in a brick-yard. These machines carry up a large quantity of water, making quite a brook running away from them, which in many instances runs long distances.

I should like to have you rise early with me some morning, and see the natives on our boat wash the deck floor. First, they throw water over it Then each man has a whisk or brush broom, laying flatwise, fastened to the under side of his right foot; and by a back and forward motion, sliding the right foot on the floor, the scrubbing is done with a vengeance. While doing this, they all sing and keep perfect time. It may not be as graceful as the dancing of our young people, but it is quite as effective. When they sing, it is, "Zallah, zallah," etc., which means in English, My God, help me.

Yesterday we called at Neneh, a place of sixteen thousand people. It is the capital of the province, and has large manufactories of pottery, supplying nearly all Egypt with gallahs and filterers. We went into the works, and saw them make their wares. A man sits with his feet in a pit. In that pit is a horizontal wheel, two feet in diameter, with a shaft running up just out of the pit. This wheel he turns with his feet. On the top of the shaft he places the clay, and spins it up with his hand, forming any shape desired. It is spun very much like plated ware, only the men in those works have tools to form the metal and run it with greater speed.

On our return we came through their bazaar. These institutions in Egypt are a curiosity.

We also visited the temple of Denderah. This is without doubt the grandest relic or ruin in all Egypt. In its day the temple must have been grand. Many of its designs are supposed to have been taken from Solomon's Temple. It is supposed to have been destroyed by the Mohammedans. The beautiful carving and sculpturing with coloring had most of them been hampered, pounded, and defaced as much as possible. We all decided that its glory in its day could not have been described with pen. The eye must have beheld it to realize its beauty and grandeur.

Luxor, or its ancient and Bible name Thebes or No, is spoken of in Ezekiel xxx. 14–16. It is a place full of historical interest, and we do not give it merely a passing notice, but are, to remain here three days, taking excursions out to the old temples, tombs, etc. It was a great city before the days of Abraham. It became the seat of empire under the eleventh and twelfth dynasties of kings. It was a walled city, said to have contained at one time five million of people.

The alluvial plains on the banks of the Nile here seem to extend her borders right and left. Standing on our boat, looking west, our eye views a beautiful plain for miles; and in the background in a crescent form rise the mountains of sandstone, which is the commencement of the Libyan desert. Then you will get a similar picture, looking east.

Thebes flourished many years. Kings became builders of heathen temples, but the day of vengeance came at last. Ptolemy Lathyrus razed it to the ground about one hundred years B.C.; and on these great plains, where once stood the great city of the world, are now scattered only ruins.

Here in Luxor is an American mission; and many of the boys and girls are studying the English language, and read quite well. We went into a gristmill to-day, said to be one of the best. They grind the wheat with a granite stone, some three and one-half feet in diameter and about four inches thick,—

that is, the upper stone,—which rests on a spindle with a small gear at the bottom. Into this is connected a large gear. The shaft of the large gear has a sweep, and to that is attached a donkey which goes round in a circle, giving the mill-stone quite a speed, and will grind nearly a bushel an hour. The owner takes the flour and sifts it by hand, and makes it into bread for sale. The wheat is plump and fine, quality of bread very good.

The obelisk that was recently set up in New York City was taken from Alexandria, where we landed on our way from Brindisi. The one erected in Paris was taken from this place. It was one of a pair. We have been looking over the remaining one and the base of the one taken away, but the one that excels them all is about two miles east of the village of Luxor. It is one piece of solid granite, one hundred and six feet high, nine feet square at the base, finely carved. Some thirty feet of the top was covered with gold, and shows the result of it to-day. This wonderful piece of work was erected by Queen Hatasu. Thus you will see that woman has outdone all the kings of the earth, and a work accomplished by her is the wonder of the world. The work on this obelisk was done in seven months and seven days.

We have been travelling over these plains about Luxor, covered with interesting relics, for the last three days; and it is wonderful what the ancient Pharaohs did, and from appearance it was for self-aggrandizement. Two miles east of Luxor stand the ruins of an immense temple. In one portion are one hundred and thirty-four pillars some fifty feet high. From this temple run several avenues, the longest extending to the river, a distance of two miles. These avenues were lined with sphinxes on each side, hundreds of them, bearing the emblem of the power of the king. Standing back of these were rows of palms and other Oriental trees.

Pharaoh had his three thousand chariots with him when he rode in state. But to-day in this region no one rides in carriages. Camels and donkeys are the modes of conveyance, excepting the sedan chair.

Farming here sticks to the fathers. They thresh the grain the old way. It is trodden out with oxen; and, to keep the old injunction good, they are not muzzled. We do not see here farm-houses as we have in New England. The people all live in villages, and go miles to do their work. You will see the Rebeccas, with their water-jars on their heads, going long distances for water. Whether these things are ever to be modernized is a hard question to answer.

IV.

CAIRO, April 2, 1895.

After mailing my last letter at Luxor on the Nile, where we spent three days, we continued our course up the river, having one hundred and thirty miles more to travel south to reach Assouan at the first cataract, where was to end our outward Nile tour. Assouan is the farthest from Springfield of any place we shall visit, and took us nearer the equator than we ever expect to be again.

The season was late to visit that tropical region, and ours was the last large party to leave the cataract this season. Hence we expected to suffer from the heat; but the Lord smiled on us, and gave us cool weather. Ninety-two in the shade was the highest the mercury went, and that was only a few hours in the middle of the day, always having cool nights. Even Vermonters can stand that temperature.

Our first stop after leaving Luxor was at Esneh, where we visited a temple which was built or had been repaired at a late date; that is, after the commencement of the Christian era. The next and only stop was at Edfu. There we visited the temple of Horace, which was modern and beautiful. Here they had patterned after Solomon's Temple, had the holy of holies with the exact measurement, also the ark of the covenant.

We reached Assouan March 24, and found it one of the prettiest towns in Upper Egypt. Here is where all the large steamers turn their prows down the river, and traffic that is going up the river is taken by camels or donkeys by the rapids, then put into small boats. This is what has built up the town, and it might well be called the offspring of the cataract. We spent two days at Assouan in the bazaars, trading and watching the habits and lives of the people, etc. We also visited the town of Philæ, giving us a donkey ride of fifteen miles. Philæ is a beautiful town at the head of the cataract. We repeated the old story of visiting another temple. This was the temple of Isis.

Some of our party returned from this place by

boat, going down the rapids in small boats managed by the natives. This was a curiosity. The natives always sing when they handle the oars. Their music has time and rhythm, and that is all there is to it.

While on the Nile, we visited one of the Nilometers. With these instruments a record of the height of the water is kept, and by this record the taxation of the crops is regulated.

Egypt is noted for its ancient historical records. Monetho, a priest and Greek scholar, was employed by Ptolemy II. to study ancient manuscript and hieroglyphics, and brought forth a work that was considered valuable at the time. A large part of this work later on was lost; but the study of the handwriting on the wall has of late years been revived, and great interest to-day is manifested in those old historical relics,— the obelisks, temples, and tombs,— and it seems as though God had made Egypt a great repository to keep the records of the Old World. With its wonderful preservative qualities, no rain or dew, a perfectly dry atmosphere, everything seems to keep in its original state. We have seen polished granite, four thousand years old, looking as clean and bright as though it had been polished within a year.

The papyrus manuscripts that have been unearthed in the temple and tombs are making revelations every day. The bread and grain brought to light, thousands of years old, are items of interest.

We have been upon the tops of some of these old temples. In one place we went up two hundred and forty-six steps. Have had some beautiful views of the Nile, with its broad plains covered with palms and fields of grain, etc.

This country is different from anything we have ever seen before. As you sail up this broad river, with its rich alluvial land on both sides, back of these plains rise somewhat abruptly hills and mountains composed largely of sandstone of a pearly gray appearance, seemingly variegated. Here commence the great sand deserts. These hills have not the first green thing on them, and are saying to the tiller of the soil, "Thus far shalt thou come, and no farther." The plains and mountains give us some beautiful sunsets.

We travelled from Cairo to Assouan, five hundred eighty-three miles; and the average width of this valley is six miles. This is all there is of Egypt excepting from Cairo to Alexandria, one hundred and thirty miles. A peculiar-shaped country, but rich in her fertility, raising two and three crops a year, and exports much more than they import. Her historical relics that are coming to light are beginning to draw tourists. Four thousand of this class have gone up and down the Nile the last year; and the number will increase in the future, giving her quite a revenue. It is a very unique trip.

If I were an artist, I would with pencil and brush give you a picture of the natives, camels, and donkeys at one of our landings. But, as I am not, I shall have to content myself with a few outlines. As soon as our boat ties up at the landing, the natives begin to gather with their wares and donkeys from all directions, trinkets to sell, donkeys to let, etc. The natives are very artistic. They clip their donkeys over the back. Then on the sides and legs they notch and slash the hair in such a way they will show beautiful palm-leaves on the sides. On their legs some of the donkeys look as though they had on short pantalets with pointed lace at the bottom, then the mitre and breastplate, etc.

Now let us take a ride into town or some objective point; and, if you are fond of fun,— and I know you are,— here is where you get it. As soon as you step ashore, and they see there is a chance to let a donkey, they will make a rush for you, every man praising up his own animal, shouting in an unknown tongue and gesticulating to the best of his ability. At first you will think you are going to have a street fight on your hands at once. Then they will begin to grab hold of you, and you will make up your mind that you are going to be quartered, and each quarter is going off on a separate donkey, and you will have four backsheesh to pay instead of one. But all is, when things begin to grow interesting, say to them, "Hands off!" and mount the first good-looking donkey you can get at, and you will be surprised to see how quickly things quiet down. No one finds any fault, and the man that secures the job is happy. The next thing is to make your donkey boy understand where you wish to go. Then you are off with a rush. The young man follows his donkey with a whip or cane, and will give you all the speed you want, using his cane over the hind parts of his animal, and shouting at top of his voice, "Zah, hoo, zah, hoo!"

but having sympathy for the donkey, and not wishing for such speed, you begin to wave your hand backward, and shout, "Slower, slower!" and, unless you are persistent in your demands, you will still keep up the rush. Either way you are sure to get there all right, then alight from your donkey and go where you please. When you return, you will find your donkey boy waiting for you. When you return to the boat and pay for your ride, it makes no difference what you give them, they will want more. The disposition with the natives is to get all they can out of the tourist. Many a time in selling their wares they will take one-eighth of what they asked in the first place. But such is life in Egypt. It is impossible to go out from the steamer into town without having from three to six of these natives following you, offering to guide you, for which they expect backsheesh, or else they are trying to sell you scarabs or some unearthly thing you care nothing about. A polite invitation for them to leave amounts to nothing. You have to go for them with a cane, and give them to understand you mean business.

The sad thing of this country is the halt, maimed, lame, and blind you meet at every turn, begging. Some of the most pitiable-looking creatures! It makes the heart sick. If a man could be a many times millionaire with a heart to give, this would be a splendid field for him.

The Nile seems to be the pride of Egypt. The people all come to it with their herds to water, also to drink themselves. Their washings are done on its shores.

Money seems to be worth more than in America, and is in smaller denominations. They have here parion, millims, and piastres. The parion is a small copper coin, value one-eighth of a cent. Two parion, a larger piece, one-fourth of a cent. The millim is very small, with silver in it, value one-half cent. Two millim, one cent. A piastre is a trifle over five cents, then there is one-half piastre. The five piastre piece, twenty-six cents, is the size of our quarter. The ten piastre piece, fifty-two cents, and twenty piastre piece, one dollar and four cents, correspond to our half-dollars and dollars. The quality of their silver is better than ours, and stands on equal footing with French gold.

We remain here about ten days, then go into Palestine, where horses take the place of donkeys.

V.

CAIRO, April 5, 1895.

The Congregational Oriental party is at this time nicely located at the D'Angleterre and new hotels that would do credit to any American city. Many of the clerks and waiters speak English, and are very polite and attentive. While we expect to remain here until the 13th, yet we are not anxious to have the hour of our departure arrive.

Cairo seems to be the Chicago of Egypt, a place of some four hundred thousand inhabitants, about twenty thousand of them English and Americans. The bulk of the residents are Mohammedans. This place was founded about A.D. 850. Touloun, a Moslem, was its first governor. In 1170 the famous Saladin usurped the throne; in 1250 the Mamelukes took possession; in 1517 it was stormed and captured by the sultan, Selim. To-day England has a powerful grip on Egypt. The khedive ran the country badly in debt. England took the bond until she stepped in, and said, "We must control the property." The Egyptian army is officered by English. In fact, they keep many of their soldiers here, and Egypt feeds them; yet England can take them away any time she chooses. The khedive lives in Cairo, and rules some six millions of people; yet he is ready to take off his hat to Johnny Bull whenever he meets him. The six millions of people in Egypt are largely Mohammedans, some half million Coptics. Here and there you will find people from Nubia, Soudan, and India. The people are a copper color, excepting those from Soudan, they being black and shiny, but, unlike the negro, have not the thick lips and curly hair. The Egyptians are straight, fine forms, white teeth; and many of them, aside from color, are handsome. They are not vicious, and are easily managed by those in authority.

The condition of women in the country is deplorable. The laws of the Mohammedans give a man a right to have four wives if he wishes for them. He buys them, the usual price being twenty-five dollars, paid for in any kind of goods the man may happen to have. If he wishes to get rid of them, the law requires him to support them nine months; and the woman has to take care of and support the children until eight years old. So you see divorce is an easy matter; and they are sure to send the wives off when they get to be old, and take ·young wives in their place. The law in these matters is a mere letter, and many of the well-to-do Arabs have twenty wives instead of four; and many times they are sent off with a piastre (five cents) instead of nine months' support. The man rides his camel or donkey, and the wife walks or runs behind. Sometimes they send them out on a two-wheel cart to air them.

The marriageable age for girls is twelve, boys eighteen. We have seen many a young wife about that age with her baby in her arms. They never educate the girls.

The laws of the Coptics are different. Only one wife is allowed.

When the prow of our steamer was headed northward on the Nile, we had but little to do upon our return but watch the scenery and the villages. There are a few towns that show thrift, with some modern-looking buildings; but the majority are the óld mud houses, and the walls are built up some seven feet high, then poles thrown across and a covering of straw to keep the sun out. Not having rain up the Nile, the roof is of minor importance. We went through many of those villages, and into some of the houses, where you will find in one room donkeys, pigs, hens, and the natives all living together; and a good, nice Vermont hog-pen is a palace to some places we saw.

There seems to be a disease of the eyes among the

children in Egypt, and the flies gather on them. We have seen children with their eyes so covered with flies you could hardly tell whether they had eyes or not; and they seem to make no effort to keep them off. This, I think, is the reason why there are so many blind people here. It is said that one in twenty is blind, either one eye or both. There are no hospitals or places for the poor, so all they can do is to sit and beg. It seems as though the condition of the people in Upper Egypt is worse than here in Cairo.

I have been wandering with you through the country. I will now try to give you a glimpse of Cairo. While there are camels and donkeys here, you will see some of the streets full of fine horses and carriages. The officers of the government and many of the wealthy have their fine turnouts. They have their sais, who are the most sylph-like beings imaginable. They can run hours without tiring. They wear a richly decorated garment, embroidered in gold arabesques, a wide silk sash with ends floating in the air, with loose gauze sleeves, white, falling to the waist, and a short skirt coming to the knees of same material. A wealthy man will have two of these men, who run abreast of each other. Sometimes you will see one alone. They carry a wand some five feet long, brought against the shoulder, when they run before the carriage. The coachman drives his team rapidly. The sais run with great speed, keeping about one hundred feet in advance, shouting to anything or anybody that is in the way to clear the track. I have never come in contact with them; but I enjoy watching them exceedingly, they look so fine and run so gracefully.

The new part of Cairo where we are located is modern in appearance, broad streets, fine public buildings, stores filled with fine-looking goods, etc.; and, if it was not for the Oriental toggery going through the streets, you would almost think you were the other side of the Atlantic.

When you leave your hotel, the first thing you meet is an Arab with a donkey. He knows a few words of English; and he says: "Fine donkey, nice donkey to ride. Donkey take you to bazaar. Fine donkey, ride easy, good donkey." No matter how strong your assertions are that you do not wish to ride, he will follow you a long distance. Another conveyance is the pasta Baluak. This annoys no one. It looks like a small street-car, seats running crosswise, so you enter on the side. The car is much wider than the running gear. There are four small wheels underneath. They hitch on a pair of horses, and go where they please in the highway. The passengers get on and off at their pleasure, paying for their ride. Very convenient where there are no horse or electric cars, things we have not seen in Egypt.

Cairo is said to have a thousand mosques. It seems to be a city of domes and minarets, some of them very handsome. We have been in several of them. They differ from the Catholic cathedrals, being entirely free from statuary, figures, or pictures. The Mohammedans are decidedly opposed to anything of the kind. In one of the squares of Cairo is a statue, upon a horse, of Abram Pasha; but, when it was erected, it met with great opposition. The alabaster mosque is one of the finest, solid columns of pure alabaster. In every one of these buildings on the east side is a circular recess, beautifully inlaid; and in this mosque this was solid onyx of the finest quality. Toward this recess every one faces when he worships: this points him toward Mecca. In the front court of this alabaster mosque is a closed fountain, some fifteen feet in diameter, with a canopy top. Around the outside are round onyx stones, about twelve inches high and twenty inches in diameter. In front of each one of these stones is a faucet. Before the man is allowed to worship in the mosque, he kneels on one of those stones, opens the faucet and washes his feet, face, head, mouth, nose, and ears. Then he enters the mosque, and performs his devotions. The floor is covered with mattings or carpets. The building is profusely lighted, having more or less colored glass, and must look fine in the evening when lighted.

We visited the oldest church in Cairo, built over one thousand years ago. It is a Coptic church, still in use. We also visited a mosque built about the same time.

Our dragoman, Hasham, is a Mohammedan; and we have a chance to study theology with him. They believe that Christ was a prophet, but Mohammed was a greater and later one. Many of them are very devoted, but their religion does not seem to bring them upon a very high plane of moral living. Hasham says he is coming to America. I have the impression that he is beginning to think that there is a better religion than he is now acquainted with.

We visited to-day the Palace Hotel, being shown all through it. This was built by the khedive for a palace, and cost eleven millions; but he found out that he had more palaces than he could support, and sold this one to a French syndicate for a hotel. The grounds are extensive, finely laid out with flowers, fountains, statuary, many beautiful trees, and about one hundred electric lights, with large globes to light the grounds in the evening, which must make it a perfect fairyland when lighted. It is located on the banks of the Nile, and their prices are from three to five dollars per day. They can take care of some two hundred, and have not been able to accommodate half that wish to stop with them. One hundred more rooms are to be added this summer. If you wish for the finest thing in Cairo, send in your name. You will not get nearer paradise in this section of country than there. We saw one arrangement that was beautiful. On some of the mirrors were painted vines and flowers, and it made it appear as though you were looking into a conservatory. It is the cheapest conservatory one can have, no danger of frost, and you will always have vines in blossom.

VI.

CAIRO, April 6, 1893.

This has been a great day in Cairo. The tomb of Mohammed in Mecca is kept covered with beautiful carpets of tapestry and embroidery, which are renewed every two years. This is the year for renewal, and they have with great labor and skill been prepared; and the 6th might be called the day of dedication. All business in Cairo came to a standstill: everybody and everything was in gay attire.

8 A.M. was the hour to meet on Citadel Hill. We were there with our carriages promptly on time. Many of those beautiful carpets were spread over oval top stretchers, carried by men. Then there was a canopy for the tomb that was gorgeous and dazzling. This was on a sacred camel, and entirely covered the animal, the top being some ten feet above the camel's back. These all passed close by our carriage. Some two thousand soldiers, with a large amount of cavalry, artillery, etc., all beautifully uniformed, and large bands of music. The khedive was in the procession. The people and carriages covered acres. The coverings for the tomb were taken from the citadel to a mosque; and in a few weeks another day will be set apart, and the goods will start for Mecca.

The night before the 6th they had what they call a feast. These goods were placed in one of the public buildings, brilliantly lighted; and eatables also were added, and all that wished went in. It was like a grand reception. When the whole thing was over, we decided we were lucky to hit so rare an occasion.

When we visited the oldest mosque, we saw the column with Mohammed's hand holding a whip imprinted on it. They claim this column flew from Mecca to Cairo,—quite a flight.

When on Citadel Hill, we saw the place where Mameluke jumped his horse off a precipice, killing his horse, but by a miracle, as it were, saved his own life. This was when Mohammed Ali made a banquet, and invited all the head men of the different provinces, and at the right moment let his soldiers in upon them, killing several hundred, this Mameluke being the only one to escape.

When Abraham walked the plains of Mamre with the angels, and pursued the captors of Lot, Egypt had her large cities, and was the centre of art and learning. Even Rome and Athens had their first instalment of knowledge and science from this old country.

Saturday we took carriages, and drove ten miles to Heliopolis. Here was located the great institution of learning in the time of Pharaoh, the place where Moses and Joseph received their education. Here is the oldest obelisk in Egypt, and the old sycamore tree, said to be growing on the spot where the holy family rested, when they went down to Egypt to escape the wrath of Herod.

The more you travel here in Egypt, the more you are impressed with its ancient historical interest.

I have given you thus far in this letter more of the new Cairo than of the old. There is a part of this city that is as ancient seemingly as are the eternal hills that are around it, and there is no way that you will get more of the Oriental life than to go with me through the bazaars. Here you will enter streets miles in length, some of them so narrow that only pedestrians and equestrians enter them. Each side is full of stalls, many of them not more than six by ten feet. On the floor is usually a rug, on which sit the merchants, many of them smoking their nargileh. These boxes or stores, and occasionally larger ones, are packed full of goods, many of the richest quality. In these bazaars you will find them manufacturing shoes, garments, silver and copper ware, etc., using the crudest tools imaginable, yet their work is fine. We saw articles in silver that were exquisite. The natives and their donkeys are going to and fro, good-naturedly jostling each other; and you can rejoice in one thing, that the large, fat people do not live in Egypt. If you are buying goods, you should pay about two-thirds the asking price. In buying expensive articles, it takes usually about three days and several cups of coffee to complete the bargain. You will find stores filled with attar of roses and the sweet-scented perfumes of Arabia and the Oriental country. The buildings usually jut over above the first story, the merchants living upstairs, the buildings so near together you can almost shake hands across the street; and, as you are aware there are acres covered in this way, you will have some idea of the wealth and stock in trade in Cairo.

While making our way through one of these

streets, we turned to our right into a narrow lane, and entered an establishment for manufacturing furniture, saw beautiful fret-work and inlaid pearl. There was a scaffold in the shop that was ten by fifty feet. We went up a ladder to get on it, and I counted forty men and boys working on that space. Some were carving, others were working on inlaid pearl; but the work which interested us most was turning beaded work. They had a fillbow, the string around the piece of wood they were turning. With one hand they kept the piece of wood in motion. With the other hand and the toes of the left foot they held the chisel, and you would be surprised to see them sit there and rapidly perform that work. I have a piece of the work in my pocket-book that I shall take to America.

In the bazaars you will see the natives selling water, lemonade, licorice water, etc. You will hear them in all directions. They have a fancy glass bottle holding about a gallon, trimmed with brass chains and dangles. This they carry on the side with a strap or chain over the shoulder. Then with two bright copper or brass saucers in one hand they strike or chime them together in a musical way, being heard a long distance, and with the cup or tumbler that is hung to the bottle will, for half a piastre, let you have all you want. I drank some of the licorice water once, but have not been dry since.

The donkeys, many of them, have a necklace around the neck with a thousand or less little brass or nickel charms or tinklets. It is very nice in these crowded bazaars; for you will hear them as they come rushing along behind you, giving you a chance to take care of number one. While you are here, you had better go through the lace, tassel, and embroidery departments where they are manufacturing these goods by hand, then, as you leave for your hotel, come through the perfumery and spice bazaars. They will give you a chance to sample their goods; and you will return with the sweet odors of Mecca, attar of roses, etc., that will be about you the rest of the day.

We have visited the ostrich farm, thirteen hundred and fifty birds, a sight to behold, saying nothing about the eggs and feathers.

Monday, the 8th, we took carriages, and drove to the Pyramids, a drive of ten miles, one of the finest roads in the country, six miles as level and straight as you could draw a line, lined each side with the libbek trees, resembling our locust. This road was built by the khedive when the Suez Canal was opened; and Empress Eugénie came here, and was the first to ride over it. We are ready to take off our hat to the empress. The pyramid we visited, and most of the party went to the top. It was some four hundred and eighty feet high, and seven hundred and sixty feet square at the base, twenty feet square at the top. On the corners the stones were laid in a way to make steps some three feet high. So two Arabs would take a person, and in a short time walk them to the top.

On our way out to the Pyramids we met two hundred and seventy camels with produce going into Cairo. Met seventy on the bridge as we cross the

Nile, twelve hundred sixty feet long. This would be quite a show if it was not in Egypt.

There are a large number of pyramids in Egypt, both small and great. These at Gizeh that we visited are the largest, and were built in the third and fourth dynasty, nothing standing to-day that dates back beyond them. Abraham, Isaac, and Jacob gazed on them probably with as much wonder as the people of to-day. There has been some speculation by different writers as to what they were built for, but there is hardly a shadow of doubt that they were built as tombs for the kings. There are many passageways and apartments in them. The ancient kings had an idea of immortality, and that the body must be preserved, in order to save the soul. Hence, as soon as they had the power, they commenced to prepare for the future. This largest pyramid was built by Cheops, and was some twenty years building. It took ten years to build the roads to transport the stone. At times there were one hundred and sixty thousand men at work on it. Cheops was a tyrant, and his subjects disliked him cordially; and, knowing this feeling to exist, he did not dare to have his body placed in this wonderful tomb or pyramid he spent so many years building. He gave orders to his few friends to have him buried in some secret place. The monument remains, but its builder is forgotten.

If you wake up to-morrow morning at four o'clock or, in fact, any morning, and your windows are open, you will hear the muezzins from all directions, calling the hour of prayer. They are in the mosques, upon the balconies of the minarets. The call lasts but a few minutes, and sounds like chanting in an unknown tongue.

We all of us seem to be creatures of circumstances. That article seemed to strike the Oriental party favorably. Yesterday we were all invited to visit the residence of one of the noted sheiks of Egypt. He is a descendant of the Prophet, is very wealthy, has four hundred houses in Cairo to rent, besides large land estates. His name is El Sadatt. He has fifty servants in his residence, some three hundred in all. He received us very cordially. We found him sitting in the court. We had an interpreter; and his servants ushered us into a large reception-room, and passed the cigarettes and coffee. Every one partook of the latter, and was invited into his gardens. The gentlemen would have been glad to have seen the ladies of the house, but that was not allowable. A eunuch was called, and took the ladies into the harem, where they found a wife and two pretty daughters, and several girl-servants, probably slaves. When we departed, we gave him our cards; and he gave each of us one of his. We returned, feeling that we had seen some of the higher life of Egypt, as well as the low.

In the evening we were invited to a reception at Dr. Grant's, who is a Scotchman. His wife was from Pennsylvania, U.S.A., and had been a schoolmate of one of our Oriental party. The doctor has been here twenty-nine years. He has a mania for collecting Egyptian relics, and his residence is a perfect museum. He read us a paper that he had prepared on Egyptian music, which was considered fine. Cer-

SHEIK EL SADATT.

tainly, it showed study. Coffee, tea, lemonade, cake, etc., were a part of the programme. We reached our hotel at 11.30 P.M., and called it a full day,

We have enjoyed our ten days' touring here in Cairo. Most of them have been busy ones. We have been pretty thoroughly through the museum, which is very extensive, but almost wholly Egyptian.

But I have had you jostling against the natives, so much on donkeys and camels, in temples and tombs, etc., so I will not detain you long in that building, but will call your attention to a few things that interest me most. First was the statue of a man, his face having a splendid expression, well formed, fine muscle and joints, well dressed for this climate, seemingly perfect in all his parts, but, when you come to inquire for his name and what material he is made from, you will discover, by close examination, that he is nothing but wood. Quite a marvel! I think Cab Ellis must have dreamed about him before he invented his jointed doll.

The 16th of February, the day we left New York, the natives found in a tomb at Doshua, up the Nile, two gold crowns of an empress, gold chains, bracelets, and all the paraphernalia for a beautiful queen. This we saw in the museum. The workmanship was exquisite, and they looked as bright as though they had just come out of a jewelry shop. The museum building was formerly a palace, built by the khedive; and parts of it are fine of themselves, and the rooms number one hundred. It also has a garden connected with it, and a part has been made zoölogical. So, when you come to Cairo, be sure and take it in. It is about three miles out of the city.

We visited while here in Cairo, the howling dervishes. Their performance is what they call worship. They howl and bend, sway in every direction; and some of them will whirl around like a top. There were about twenty of them on a platform; and some fifty people went in to see them, with admission fee. The question with me was which was the bigger fools, the audience or the performers.

Saturday we leave here for Port Saïd by rail, there take the boat for Jaffa, and then to Jerusalem, which place we shall probably reach about the middle of next week; and I will write you from that place.

While stopping here in Cairo, we have seen some American reminders. You will occasionally see a bicycle, have seen one steam-roller for making roads. A part of the streets have on them the water-cart sprinklers. In other parts of the city what is done in that line is done with the leather water-bottle that we read of in ancient Bible history. It is the skin of the goat, many of them with the hair on, and being sewed up, from appearance, will hold two or three pailfuls. They are filled and emptied at the neck, which has a small' opening. You will see thousands of the natives at the Nile filling these bottles. I should say they would weigh, when filled, one hundred pounds. They are carried on the side with a strap over the shoulder. They will go on the street, partly close the outlet with one hand, giving a swaying motion, and will thus sprinkle the streets quite rapidly and very acceptably to the dusty traveller; yet, when you have summed up the whole country, you will be obliged to write the word *passé*. They

WATER BOTTLES AND FILTERS OF EGYPT.

are ploughing with the same plough that Elisha used, treading out the grain with oxen. The camels are the burden-bearers. Everything about as it was four thousand years ago. Whether Jonah's experience, as related by Dudley Warner, had any effect upon them, I am not prepared to say. When the whale landed Jonah on shore, his skin tender as a parboiled chicken, he saw a blind man eating dates. Jonah with his tender heart restored the man's eyesight. As soon as this was done, he began to snap the seed at Jonah, and, he being in a tender condition, it hurt him prodigiously, and he complained to the Lord; but word soon came back to let things be as he had fixed them or take the consequences.

The Egyptians have let things be about as they were, and when they are going to have courage to change them no one can tell. A new civilization will have to be introduced, woman elevated, Mohammedanism exchanged for a pure religion.

LETTERS FROM THE HOLY LAND.

I.

JAFFA, SYRIA, April 15, 1895.

We left Cairo the 13th at 11.30, ran out on the main line to Alexandria, some twenty miles, then branched off, running due north through the land of Goshen, a beautiful, rich farming country of broad plains, as fine as anything we have seen in Egypt. This was where Pharaoh told Joseph to locate his kindred, and where the Israelites grew and multiplied, and afterwards became slaves, and were at last obliged to make bricks without straw; and then Moses came, and led them out to the land of Canaan.

We passed through some of the treasure cities they built for Pharaoh. One of the places is now named Zakayik. After leaving this, we passed along the edge of the great desert with nothing but sand and sage brush.

We also passed Tel-el-Kiber, where the battle between the English and Egyptians was fought in 1882. The English soldiers being so far superior, much better drilled and equipped, they made quick work of the affair, the battle lasting only twenty-five minutes, the English losing only twenty-six men. We saw the little plat of ground where they were buried, which was fenced in and neatly cared for. As soon as the battle was over, the cavalry proceeded at once to Cairo, and made their demands, which were granted without further resistance.

About five o'clock we reached Ismalia, where we changed cars, taking a narrow-gauge road to Port Saïd, forty miles distant. Ismalia is noted for its baggage thieves; for, if a piece of baggage is lost there, it is never found again. So we held on to our grips, and kept our eyes on the trunks, which had to be transferred about ten rods from one depot to another. This was done by Arabs taking them on their backs, which was a marvel to us. I saw one Arab with four steamer trunks on his back at once. I would not have believed such a story, had I not seen it with my own eyes, and shall not insist on any of my friends taking any stock in this transportation company unless they choose to do so.

Ismalia is where we strike the Suez Canal, and is about half-way between Port Saïd and Suez. Our train follows the canal all the way to Port Saïd.

The earth that was taken out of the canal was largely taken out with baskets by the natives, and left on the banks. This seems queer to a Yankee, but labor at ten cents a day changes the operation wonderfully. Much of the way we could not see the water in the canal, and it was a peculiar sight to see steamers of all sizes sailing through the sandy desert. At times we could only see the upper part of the vessel.

This great water-way cost nineteen million pounds sterling, some over twelve million being taken by the stockholders, and the rest by the khedive. The income is getting to be enormous. The first year,

1871, the receipts were three hundred and forty thousand pounds. In 1890 they were two million six hundred and eighty-nine thousand pounds. The canal has a depth of twenty-six feet, and at the bottom is some seventy feet wide. Within a few years the electric search-light has been introduced, which enables the vessels to run nights.

We reached Port Saïd at eight o'clock in the evening, and such a motley crowd you never saw. From the chatter and clamor that was going on we thought that the Tower of Babel must be somewhere near. We took carriages, and went to the Eastern Exchange, a hotel seven stories high, fireproof, with a twenty-foot wide veranda running all around the building. This was carried up the seven stories; and most of the rooms opened on to those verandas, and in this climate, and standing on the seashore, was very pleasant.

Port Saïd has some twenty-three thousand inhabitants, and is said to be one of the wicked places of Egypt. The next day after our arrival was Easter Sunday, and you would have thought it was the Fourth of July,— bands of music, firing of cannon, and a general holiday. We remained in our hotel until about four o'clock, then went aboard a large French steamer that lay in front of the hotel, and at about 6 P.M. steamed out of the bay for Jaffa, reaching this place about eight o'clock in the morning.

To-morrow morning at six we start for Jerusalem. Some of our company are going by carriages, others on horseback.

Jaffa, or the Bible name Joppa, is where Jonah

started from, when he came in contact with the whale.

As you come up the bay, you see the city commencing at the water's edge, towering up as it recedes, one tier of buildings above another. Follow this up some ten minutes' walk, and you come up on a broad plain, a place of some twenty thousand people, about one-half Mohammedans, the other half from all creation, nearly all kinds of dress but American. Most of that is seen on the tourist. The bazaars are fearful; that is, as far as dirt is concerned. Jaffa is the shipping port for Jerusalem. Here was landed the material in the time of Solomon for the building of the temple.

Our hotel is located on the east side of the city, and is a very comfortable place to stop at. On the upper veranda you can look over hundreds of acres of orange-trees, and far in the distance can be seen the hills of Judea.

We have visited the house where Dorcas made so many garments, also the house of Simon the tanner, where Peter had his vision when praying on the house-top. Have driven out some two miles to a German settlement, and found a beautiful country, more variety than in Egypt.

Jaffa has no harbor for large steamers, so we had to be landed in small boats. There are times when the surf is so high that they cannot land the passengers, and they carry them by to Beyrout; but we were fortunate, and were landed very nicely, although some of our party were fearful that they should go to the bottom of the sea. But after we were in the little boats, and went tossing up and down over the waves, we rather enjoyed it.

One peculiarity of this country, there is no wharfage. We find the climate a little cooler than on the Nile, and more variety of scenery. Here we first placed our feet on the land of Palestine. This was the section of country allotted to the tribe of Dan.

II.

JERUSALEM, April 17, 1895.

Monday evening, the 15th, at Jaffa, our managers gave notice that we should be called the next morning at 4.30, to have our trunks and grips packed and be ready for breakfast at 5.30, and we would start at 6 for Jerusalem, forty miles, over one of the best roads to be found in any country. The party had the privilege of choosing, go by carriage and make the journey in one day, or on horseback, taking two days for the trip. There were fourteen that chose carriages, the members from Springfield being among the number. Prompt on time, with four carriages and our dragoman, we bade good-by to Jaffa, one of the oldest cities in the world, and headed our horses eastward toward Mount Zion, driving several miles through orange and lemon groves, until we struck the plains of Sharon. (See Song of Solomon ii. 1.) We found a beautiful country, with a profusion of roses and flowers as far as the eye could reach. We passed at our right a Jewish agricultural college, established by Charles Netter, of Paris. A little farther on at the left a modern village, said to be on the site of ancient Hazar-shual, where Samson caught the three hundred foxes (Judges xv. 4); and by the way we met a young Rev. Mr. Green, who used to preach at Hartford, Vt. He has been in this region a few weeks, roaming the country, gathering flowers. He thinks there would be no trouble now in catching that number of foxes, as in many places you can almost knock them over with a club. They are' called jackals. They were about our hotel at Jaffa, and stirred up the dogs, so that between the dogs and jackals we were kept awake half the night.

The next place of importance was Ramleh, the traditional Aramathea. (See Matt. xxvii. 57.) Here is a stone tower, said to have been built by the Crusaders. It is some one hundred feet high. We went to the top, and had a grand view from Gaza on the south, to Mount Carmel on the north, eastward the land of Judah and Benjamin, westward the Mediterranean. Looking south-west, you see Ashdod Gath, the home of Goliath. Farther to the east you see Gezer, a Canaanitish town taken by Pharaoh and presented to his daughter, Solomon's wife.

After leaving Ramleh, we pass at our left Gimzo, which was taken from the Israelites by the Philistines. Six miles from Ramleh we go down into the valley of Ajalon, where Joshua commanded the moon to stand still. (See Joshua x. 12.) This valley runs north and south, and is perhaps one mile across, with a depth of one hundred feet or more below the plains. Each side beyond this valley we pass the village of Latron, said to be the home of the penitent thief. Latron is about half-way from Jaffa to Jerusalem. In leaving this, we go down into the Wady Ali, and then begin to climb the hills of Judah, and soon enter the land of Benjamin and pass the old site of Kirjath-jearim, where the ark of God rested for twenty years. If you will cast your eye to the left, you will see in the distance, upon the top of a conical hill, Mizpah, the highest land in this part of Palestine. This was where Saul was chosen king. (See 1 Samuel x. 17-24.) Gibeah of Saul is in sight, also the home of John the Baptist. From this place we pass down through another valley and around the brow of the hill. Beyond we come in sight of Jerusalem, only about one mile distant.

The last ten miles was a continual climb most of the way, and I have never been so impressed with the Scripture where it speaks of the tribes going up to the Holy City to attend their great religious festivals. Last Sunday was Easter, and there was a great celebration in Jerusalem. We were on the road Tuesday, and it was full of people returning from that festival. We met one company of about one hundred. Some were walking, and others riding on horses, donkeys, or camels. We were told that the party would be away from home sixty days, thirty days each way.

You would see horses with a pillion on them, straps going over the horse's back holding boxes on each side, perhaps a little canopy over the boxes. In these boxes were the little children, and the mother sitting on the pillion, the husband walking behind. Then would come a camel, with the mother riding, and the children in front of her. There were all kinds and ways, nags and Arabs, a motley crowd.

The country about Jerusalem is different from what I had pictured it. It is very mountainous for a long distance westward, and the hills have a very peculiar appearance. The sides of these hills and mountains look as though human agencies had been at work on them, and terraced them from bottom to top. They will show a line of stone from two to four feet high running along the side of the hill, as straight as a line, then grass or trees for several rods, then another layer of stones, so on up to the top. The olive orchards many times extend clear to the tops of the mountains. The gray stone and the green give in the distance a mottled appearance.

It seems to be a great field for goats. We saw hundreds of them as we came up the mountain, every flock having a shepherd.

As we near Jerusalem, and are near the top of the mountain, our eyes behold wonderful beauty in the landscape in all directions. Jerusalem is an elevated city. "And as the mountains are around about Jerusalem," etc.,—the saying is a true one; but the mountains are not high ones, for the city itself towers toward heaven, and you have to descend into a valley before you can climb any of the surrounding mountains.

On our arrival at Jerusalem we went to the Jerusalem hotel which is in the new part of the city, outside of the city walls of old Jerusalem, and is beautiful for situation.

The horseback party arrived the next day after

our arrival, and pitched their tents not far from our hotel, but near the Jaffa gate. We were to have two camping tours, the short one from this place and return, occupying three days, going to Jericho, the Jordan and Dead Sea, distance thirty miles. This is considered the most dangerous travelling we shall have. As it was in the time of Christ, so it is now, full of Bedouins and robbers. Being entirely an unsettled country, our orders were to keep together. If any one went ahead or lagged behind, he would do so at his own risk.

It is necessary to have some official on this trip. So we had a son of one of the sheiks, mounted on his gray charger, armed to the teeth; and our dragomen all had their short swords. This camping business is a regular circus, a picnic every day. It takes about one hundred horses, mules, and forty men to move us. Those at the hotel were to take horses, and partake of the luncheon, in tent, with the others; but at night we were to be at the hotel in Jericho. There are two hotels, the Jordan and the Bellevue. We went to the latter, a small house, but very neat, and Oriental from the word go. We were there two nights; and I, for one, should have been glad to have stayed longer. The only out was that the dogs and jackals made things lively nights. One gentleman of our party got up, and shouted out of the window for them to get out of the way and stop their noise, but the effect, seemingly, was to wake up more dogs, and the music was increased instead of being diminished; but I am rather a friend of the canines, and those troubles rest very lightly on my shoulders.

SON OF A SHEIK

Now, if you would like a dim picture of this first camping tour, you had better meet me at the Jerusalem hotel early Thursday morning, April 19. First there was an array of saddle horses brought into the yard for us to select from, grays, bays, and blacks. The members from Springfield chose a pair of bay geldings that had been used to following each other. We have two ladies that cannot endure the horseback riding, and have palanquins.

About 6.30 A.M. the straps were all buckled, and we were on our horses, moving down toward the Jaffa gate, where we met the rest of the party; and then we moved north outside the old walls, passing the Damascus gate, then turning east, which brings us into the valley of Kedron or Jehosaphat, as it is sometimes called. Passing along the edge of Gethsemane, look up at the right, and you have a fine view of the eastern wall of Jerusalem. At the left you look up Mount Olivet, and see the road David went barefooted, when he fled the city in time of Absalom's rebellion. We passed the place where Stephen was stoned, the pool of Siloam, Absalom's tomb, also the tomb of Zechariah.

Through this section we encountered the greatest number of lepers and beggars in the most pitiable condition, sitting beside the roadway, pouring forth their cries and lamentations. But we are soon past all this, and begin to wind our way around the brow of Olivet. In less than an hour from starting we are at the little village of Bethany, which is located the other side of the Mount of Olives from Jerusalem. Here seems to be a valley coming up from the south; and at the head of this valley, in a semicircle, lies nestled the little town of Bethany, at the foot of Mount Olivet. We saw the spot where Martha, Mary, and Lazarus lived, saw the tomb of the latter, could almost feel on our brow the warm Christian atmosphere that pervaded that place more than eighteen hundred years ago, that made it so attractive to the Saviour of mankind. We were pointed out the place where Simon the leper lived.

From this place to Jericho, some eighteen miles, we pass only one place where anybody lives. Jericho, located on the plains of the Jordan, is four thousand feet lower than Jerusalem, hence the expression "going down to Jericho."

The plains of the Dead Sea are thirteen hundred feet lower than the ocean, and is the lowest land in the world. As we pass on from Bethany, we go winding our way down those narrow ravines, hills and mountains each side, with many caves for the robbers. On the side of these mountains are the shepherds, with their flocks of goats and sheep. About half-past ten we come to the only residence on the road, being on a somewhat elevated spot. Here we stop for lunch. Tradition says here was the inn where the Samaritan left the wounded man. We took little stock in that. However, we laid a man across a donkey's back, with a good Samaritan standing beside him, and got a snap shot at them with a kodak. With our lunch we had water taken from the brook Cherith.

Soon after we started, we visited the spot where Elijah was fed by the ravens.

From this time to the Jordan valley the mountains and hills looked arid and barren, having a chalky appearance; and the gorges along which we passed were fearfully deep, and had, no doubt, been cut down by the water.

About four o'clock we reached the plain, turned to the left, and went up to the fountain of Elisha, that he healed of its bitter qualities. This is near the mountains, boils up from the ground, running away quite a large stream. We were thirsty, and drank heartily, finding a good quality of water. Here is supposed to be the old site of Jericho, which was shaken down, and a curse pronounced on any one that should attempt to rebuild. There was any amount of stones and rubbish about there, but we saw nothing of any rams' horns.

About a mile south of this place is the Jericho of Christ's day, with some new buildings added. We were shown an old stone house, or the ruins of one, that is claimed to be the house of Zaccheus. They also pointed out the tree he climbed to see the Lord. It might have been a descendant from the original one, but that is as far as we should care to go.

At Jericho we stopped for the night, some in hotels, others in tents.

Friday our day's work was to go to the shore of the Dead Sea, and from there to the banks of the river Jordan, where the children of Israel crossed, and Elijah divided up the waters as he went up in his chariot, also where Christ was baptized. We found the Dead Sea a beautiful sheet of water, clear as crystal. Some of the party went in bathing. It is said to contain some fifteen per cent. more salt than the ocean, and is heavier per cubic foot than the human body. From these plains you can see across the sea and river the hills of Moab, Mount Nebo and Pisgah, where Moses was allowed to go to look into the promised land. We took our lunch on the banks of the Jordan, had the water from the river to drink. Some crossed the river, which is about a hundred feet wide and quite swift in its current, in boats. On our return to Jericho for the night we crossed the old site of Gilgal, where the children of Israel first camped, also the valley of Achor, where Achan and family were stoned. If the deed had to be done, they could not have found a better place; for there is plenty of material close at hand.

The plains of the Jordan are not as fertile as we expected to find them, not like the Nile valley. They are probably worn out, and were more fertile in the days of Abraham and Lot; for here was the place where Abraham told Lot to choose which way he would go, and he, seeing the well-watered plains of Jordan, pitched his tent toward Sodom, the location of which was where the Dead Sea now is, or plains this side. If it were sunk, then the sea is the place; but there is an appearance of a ruined city this side on the plain, and I think we had better call that the spot. In either case the mountains are near at hand where Lot went for safety.

Saturday we were in the saddle early, and continued our return until we reached Bethany. Met on our way the Prince and Princess of Germany. They

CROSSING THE JORDAN.

were going over the same route we had just taken. We stopped some two hours for lunch at Bethany. Then, instead of going around the brow of the Mount of Olives as we came, we went over the old road, over the top, and came down the same pathway the Saviour came on his triumphal entry, and where he wept as he beheld the city in its wickedness, from the Mount of Olives. You get a fine view of the city.

There has been a church built within a few years, beside it a very high tower. Up this tower we went, giving us a view of the whole surrounding country. At the base of Olivet we visited the Garden of Gethsemane, then followed down the valley of Kedron, to where the valley of Hinnom intercepts it, then up the Gihon valley to our hotel. This took us entirely around the walled part of the city. While at lunch at Bethany, some soldiers went by with some robbers that had been captured, that were chained together, walking. The soldiers were on horseback, taking them to prison.

Sunday, the 21st, has been a day of rest. The Congregational party held service at 9.30 on Mount Calvary, a small elevation just outside the city walls. Rev. Mr. Clark, of Salem, Mass., conducted the services, which were very impressive. The American consul, Mr. Wallace, a young gentleman, and his wife were there, and at the close spoke beautifully. At the foot of Mount Calvary is a plot of ground that evidently was at one time used for a garden. By excavating an embankment at the end of this garden, some two years ago, General Gordon discovered a tomb that has every evidence of being the tomb where Christ was laid. While there was room for four, there never had been but one of the niches occupied; and the top or stone cover of this had never been sealed. Christ, you know, was anointed for burial. Had he not risen, this covering stone would have been sealed. While the Mohammedans have his tomb in the city, yet we know the Scriptures do not warrant any such thing. Jerusalem has nothing that will impress the Bible scholar as Calvary and the tomb at the head of this garden. We remain here until Wednesday, going to Bethlehem, and return Tuesday.

About one year ago there was much in the daily papers in America about a strange young man from the West that had made a wager of $10,000 that he would go to Jerusalem in twelve months' time, starting without a cent of money, and would not ask for money the whole distance. He started from Galveston, Tex. I never even dreamed of seeing this strange young man, as he was called; but, strange as it may seem, he put in an appearance at the Jerusalem Hotel last Saturday. He has been on the road ten months and twenty days. His name is P. P. Killiner, is a regular cow-boy, has leather suit of clothes, made by the Indians out of antelope skins, with fringes of leather on all the seams. He has walked thirty-five hundred miles, sold his photograph, letting people pay him whatever they pleased. They got up quite an excitement over him in New York, and gave him money enough to cross the ocean. When he went down to take the boat, they crowded the street so full it was impossible to move. He attended services with the Congregational party Sunday, and went with them over Mount Moriah Monday.

III.

JERUSALEM, April 22, 1895.

Bethlehem is one of the old landmarks of Palestine, full of historical interest. This was the home of David's relations, and is located some six miles south of Jerusalem, and is about the same height above the sea as the hill of Zion. As you leave the Jaffa gate, you pass down and across the valley of Gihon, coming up near the hill of Evil Counsel (so called because at that place they took counsel against Christ), and soon are on the plain of Rephaim, where David fought the Philistines; and, judging from the broad sweep of the plain, it must have been a hand-to-hand fight. Here is where David refused to drink the water he so thirsted for, brought from the spring near Bethlehem, because it was done at the risk of the lives of his men that procured it.

Before I take you any further, it might be well for you to look at the surrounding country of Jerusalem. If you stand on the hill of Zion (or perhaps a better place would be the Mount of Olivet), no one point of compass will attract the eye more than looking south toward Bethlehem. As I have told you before, the country here is made up of hills and valleys, elevations and depressions, rugged and rocky at that, yet the mingling of the olive, almond, fig, orange, and lemon groves, gives it a beauty that attracts the eye; and, while you cannot see Bethlehem from where you are standing, yet, if drawn by the love of the beautiful, your first outing from the city will be in that direction. I have given you a view from a distance. When you plant your feet on this beautiful country my eye has taken in, you will exclaim, "My, how rocky!"

After we leave the plain of Rephaim, we come to the tomb of Rachel. For a wonder the Mohammedans, Greeks, and Latins all worship Rachel; and the day we went to Bethlehem was a special day, and they were all rushing to the tomb to weep for her. The tomb is a white building, standing close to the travelled road, the front an arched portico or entrance. Then you step down some half-dozen steps into a square apartment, perhaps twenty feet each way. In the centre is built up the receptacle for the body, six feet high, eight feet long, four feet wide, giving a chance to pass around it. Here the people come with their Hebrew Bibles, reading Jacob's lamentation, and crying as if their poor hearts would break, kissing the tomb, etc. They remain a short time, and then others take their places. We passed around with others, but could not in so short a time get into the spirit of the worship.

In passing through this country as well as Egypt, the traditions and the queer things the ignorant people will show and relate to you about the old saints and prophets will make you tired.

For example, just beyond Rachel's tomb is a flat

rock ; and it looks as though a man had been on his back and had sunk into the stone some four inches. The people will show it to you, and tell you it was where Elijah slept the first night after he fled from Jezebel. This is only one of the many foolish things they have on the brain. But, if you will take profane and religious history in one hand and common sense in the other, you will find things that will interest you at every turn you make, and will have all you can carry away with you.

A little farther on we turn to the left, and in a short time are at Solomon's pools. They are three in number, built by the wise man ; and from these the water was taken into Jerusalem.

From the pools we drove to Bethlehem, a place of some eight thousand people, largely Christians. They are tillers of the soil. Herding of cattle is a large business with them. They manufacture rosaries, crosses, and other fancy articles in wood, mother-of-pearl, and stone from the Dead Sea. It is quite a market town for the Bedouins and peasants from the surrounding country. There is a very old church built over the spot where Christ was born, and they will show you the place where Joseph was when the angel warned him to flee into Egypt.

We visited an underground apartment, or nearly so, where Saint Jerome translated the Hebrew Bible into the Latin (the Vulgate). Saint Jerome was born of pagan parents in 331, and was afterward baptized at Rome. While journeying in the East, he had a vision at Antioch, commanding him to renounce the study of heathen writers, which he did, and finally took up his abode at Bethlehem. Here you will see a painting of him, with a Bible in his hand. Joab, Asahel, and Abishai once resided here at Bethlehem. (See 2 Samuel ii. 18.) In the eyes of the prophets Bethlehem was especially sacred as the home of the family of David, but the one great and lasting triumph for that little town was the birth and humble beginning of one who is to conquer sin.

IV.

Some four hundred and fifty years after Joshua led the children of Israel through the divided waters of the Jordan, and with his military forces swept up the Jordan valley and up through the hills of Judea, destroying those heathen nations,— when these four hundred and fifty years had been placed on the tablet of time King David appeared on the scene, with Joab as his major-general. Mount Zion was then called Jebus, and the people were called Jebusites.

King David made an attack, capturing the city, Joab being the first man to enter.

Josephus claims that Melchizedek once lived here. On Mount Zion David built his palace, this being the whole of the city.

Thirty-seven years later the foundation of the temple was laid on Mount Moriah. These two elevations are divided by the Tryphon valley, and were at one time connected by a bridge.

On Mount Moriah Ornan had his threshing-floor, and it was also the spot where Abraham offered up

Isaac. Mount Zion became the civil capital of the nation, and Mount Moriah the sacred capital. Jerusalem attained its greatest power during Solomon's reign, but this was largely lost by the revolt of Jeroboam.

It passed through many changes of fortune, until five hundred and eighty-eight years before Christ, when it was destroyed by Nebuchadnezzar, and the Jews were taken into captivity. Jerusalem remained a heap of ruins until Cyrus allowed the Jews to return, guided by Ezra and Nehemiah, and for many years, until Grecian power became strong in Western Asia, Syria and Palestine were governed by Persian satraps in Damascus; yet the Jewish priest had much liberty.

Some three hundred and thirty years before Christ, after the battle of Issus, Palestine fell under the dominion of Alexander the Great. That illustrious monarch appeared one day before Jerusalem on the hills to the north-west, where now stand the Russian buildings; and a solemn procession, headed by the high priest, clad in pontifical robe, marched out to meet him. As soon as the monarch saw them, he advanced, and reverently saluted the sacred name inscribed on the priest's mitre, saying, "I adore not the man, but the God with whose priesthood he is honored. When in Macedonia, pondering how to subdue Asia, I saw this figure in a dream, and he encouraged me to advance, promising to give me the Persian empire. I look upon this as an omen that I have undertaken the expedition by divine command, and success will be mine." Alexander granted the Jews many privileges; and after his death Jerusalem fell into the hands of the Ptolemies of Egypt, under whose mild rule it remained over two hundred years, when it was plundered and defiled by Antiochus Epiphanes. Two years later he sent his general, Apollonius, to complete the work; and all the able-bodied men were slain, and the women and children sold into slavery.

Then arose the priestly family of Asmones to revenge their injuries and vindicate the honor of their God. This warfare lasted until thirty-four years before Christ, when Herod the Great was appointed ruler of the Jews. In the year 70 the Romans stormed the city, and killed more than a million Jews (this number is given by Josephus), and razed the temple to the ground.

Wars and fighting went on until 636, when Omar captured the city, and ordered the mosque of Omar built. Jerusalem was taken by the Crusaders in 1229; and in 1243 it was secured by the Moslems, and has been in their power ever since. The last few years the Jews have been returning, and have settled largely outside the city walls at the north-west. The Russian Jews have some fine buildings. Within the walls the city is dirty. Many of the streets are arched, and lined with bazaars. Zion Street runs from the Jaffa gate through the city. David Street is another of the main streets. The city seems divided into four sections, each section being occupied by different religious sects,— Mohammedans, Latins, Christians, and Armenians. The city is poorly watered, only two nearly dried up fountains they depend on. Cisterns catch the water from the roofs of the buildings. Lumber is a scarce article. The buildings are nearly all stone; and, from appearances, the inhabitants of that country are more efficient in working on stone than on any other material. The stones in the old walls of Jerusalem, laid without mortar or cement, are fitted so closely that you can hardly tell where they are joined together,— perfect joints. From the Mount of Olives you get the finest view of the city. It is composed of four elevations, Mount Moriah, Zion, Ackra, and Bezetha, the two former lying to the east and the most prominent, and rich with historical interest. No city in the world so thrills the soul as the one that has within its bosom Mount Zion and Mount Moriah. While you may not believe all that the native tells you about the exact localities of the thrilling scenes of eighteen hundred years ago, yet you know you are near the spot where the King of kings yielded to the will of the Father, triumphed over death, led captivity captive, and established a kingdom that Satan has not been able to prevail against. You can go to the house of Caiphas where they took Christ the night of the betrayal. They will show you where Peter sat when he denied his Master. From there it is not very far to Pilate's judgment hall. When that was rebuilt, it is evident they dug down to the old foundation; and you can, no doubt, stand where Christ stood when before Pilate, you can see the stone upon which Pilate stood when he pronounced judgment. This building is now occupied by the Latin Sisters. They will also show you the way

Christ was led out to be crucified, where he fell with the cross, where he spoke to the women and told them not to weep for him, but weep for themselves, etc.

On Mount Moriah stood Solomon's temple and palace, said to cover — with all its courts and appendages — acres, some say thirty. The mosque of Omar now stands on Mount Moriah. Though not so large as the temple, yet its symmetrical architecture, beautiful stained glass, tiling, etc., will fill you with admiration. There is no mosque in the Turkish empire that surpasses it in beauty.

In the mosque is the dome of the rock, with its steps leading up to it, with the hole in the centre where the blood went in time of sacrifice, being connected by a subterranean passage to the Kedron valley. This rock is fifty-seven by forty-three feet, and six and one-half feet high. It is held wonderfully sacred by the Mussulmans. They claim that Mohammed went up from this rock, and the rock started to follow him; but the angel Gabriel put his hand on it, and stopped it. The Armenian convent, one of the largest buildings in the city, is said to hold eight thousand. We were shown the Church of St. James, said to mark the site where he was killed by Herod (Acts xii. 1, 2). It contains his tomb and chair, also three stones, one from Mount Sinai where Moses received the law, one from the Jordan where the children of Israel crossed, and one from Mount Tabor where, some think, the transfiguration took place. Near the Damascus gate you can enter a subterranean passage where there have been

THE JEWS' WAILING-PLACE

thousands upon thousands of stone quarried here. You take lights, and walk miles under the city. Stone has been taken out here for building and rebuilding Jerusalem. You can enter a building in which is David's tomb, which they will not allow you to see; but you may visit a room above, called the Cœnaculum. It is fifty by thirty feet; and here it is claimed that Christ instituted the Lord's Supper, where the apostles were gathered on the day of Pentecost, when Peter in his sermon referred to the tomb of David as being with them (Acts ii. 29).

You can take Baedeker or a good guide with you, and travel days in the city with great interest.

Friday is the day to visit the Jews' wailing-place in the Tyropœon valley, by the walls of the city, and near where the temple stood. Here they read the old prophecies and promises, and weep, to all appearances, from the bottom of their hearts, evidently sincere mourners over the destruction of their city, and the scattering of their people to the four corners of the earth. They believe, no doubt, that they are to be gathered together, and re-established in the Holy City some time in the future.

Jerusalem is situated high upon the hills of Judah, with her foundations of granite; and, as you stand on Olivet, you view her palaces and the surrounding country, with its hills ribbed with lime-rock, granite, and marble, and you admire it, for it was once the Holy City. But I am confident, if David had seen old Vermont clothed in her beautiful garments as she is in summer time, he would never have settled down in Jerusalem.

But the die was cast, and Jerusalem was and is to be the religious centre of the world. Around it clusters sacred memories. From its Mount Calvary went forth a power that rent the rocks asunder. From this centre went forth the great reformation and the uplifting of the nations of the earth. It is a joy to every Christian to stand on Olivet, to walk through the Garden of Gethsemane, and over Calvary and Mount Zion: it will add a richness to the study of the holy Scriptures. It is an old saying, "See Naples, and die." There is a mistake. The phraseology should be different: "Don't die, unless you are obliged to, until you have seen Naples." I would say the same in regard to Palestine and the Holy Land.

Our stay in and about Jerusalem has been exceedingly interesting, and we shall study the Scriptures with greater interest than ever before.

We start the 24th on our long camping tour from here to Beyrout. I shall write up as I go along the route, but shall not mail it until we reach our destination, which will be May 11.

V.

APRIL 25, 1895.

Early in the morning of the 24th, at Jerusalem, we headed our horses due north, commencing our long camping tour of eighteen days from Jerusalem to Beyrout, getting a view of old historic relics and towers that cannot be reached in any other way; that is, over a road that is either foot or horseback, and hotels are rocky, few, and far between.

After crossing the Kedron valley, we commenced to climb hills and descend into valleys, and soon were on what is called the Damascus road; that is, if it can be called a road. Our first elevation was over Mount Scopus. Here was where Titus's camp was pitched. Here the doom of the Holy City was decreed. We thought of the holy family pursuing their way from the great religious festivals to Nazareth. We passed Bier, where tradition says the holy child was first missed.

Our first halt was some two miles out from Jerusalem, at the tombs of the kings; and, as we proceeded on our journey, we found the ascending and descending growing in steepness, the rocks and ledges fearful. We thought of General Putnam riding down the stone steps, and decided that we could put the general in the shade. The horses here are trained for these roads, and are sure-footed. Let them have the reins, and they will take you to the bottom of the hill in safety, over places you would hardly dare go down on foot. The horses are shod with a flat shoe that nearly covers the whole foot, and it is a mystery how they stand on the ledges as they do. Woe to the man that attempts to ride an American horse over the roads we have travelled!

As we passed on from Mount Scopus, we see to our right, upon a hill-top, the town of Ramah, where Samuel was born and buried. Farther on we passed the town of Ophrah, the home of Gideon, but saw nothing of the men that lapped water. About eleven o'clock we go down into the valley, and find our lunch-tent pitched in a green place, once a reservoir, and find it to be the town of Bethel. Here was the spot where Abraham and Jacob watered their flocks, and Jacob set up the pillar of stones at this place. Here was where Jeroboam set up his false worship, which proved a thorn in the sides of the Jewish kings, having an unfriendly capital so near Mount Zion, with the golden calf ready to attract the loose-minded.

The ways of sin are always more attractive than the ways of righteousness to the thoughtless and indifferent.

We rested ourselves and horses here some two hours, and then were in the saddle four hours, bringing us into a pleasant valley, near a little town without historic interest, and where we tented for the night. *Table d'hôte* was good, and a good night's rest was the verdict in the morning; and we moved on, and soon halted at Shiloh, located on high ground, commanding a fine view. Here was where the ark of God rested twenty years; and here was where Eli died. All there is left to-day are foundation walls, ruins, and an historic name. We found the travelling better to-day than the day we started, which we enjoyed as travellers in a strange land.

While we were upon the mountains a part of the time, yet we passed through some beautiful valleys. Rev. Mr. Green, formerly of Hartford, Vt., to whom I have referred before as a botanist, travelling here, informed us that there were fifteen hundred varieties of wild flowers. The fields of Palestine are full of them. In many places you will see beautiful green tapestry, full of flowers. This might be called the flowery kingdom; and we got many beautiful landscape views.

On we ride, feasting our eyes; and at twelve o'clock we halt at Jacob's well for lunch. Here was where the Saviour talked with the women of Samaria, where he spoke to his disciples of the fields being ripe for the harvest; and we imagined he saw the fields as we can see them to-day. As you stand at the well, facing east, you have thousands of acres of beautiful plain land before you, covered with waving grain nearly ready for the sickle. We halted at this lovely spot some three hours. A few minutes' walk north from our tent brings you to the tomb of Joseph, who was the son of Jacob. You well remember that his bones were brought here and buried. We have been travelling north through historic grounds, where the old patriarchs had roamed with their herds, passed the town of Dothan, where Jacob sent his son Joseph to look after his brothers, and crossed the track of the caravan going to Egypt, taking Joseph with them. It has been a panorama of historical events.

When we are in the saddle again, we turn square to the left, going west, down through the narrow valley of Shechem, passing between Mount Gerizim on our left and Mount Ebal on the right. Here was where the people stood in the valley, and the blessings were pronounced from Mount Gerizim, and the cursings from Mount Ebal, and the people said, "Amen." Principles declared there that have held good ever since,— The ways of righteousness are easy, but the ways of sin are hard. Here was where the people asked Rehoboam for more clemency; but the foolish boy discarded the counsel of the older men, and told them that his father had chastised them with whips, but he would with scorpions.

About one hour's ride, and we were at Nablous, the old town of Shechem, where we found our tents pitched in a beautiful olive grove; and we turned in for the night, being well satisfied with our day's work, this being the spot and place, as you will see by the date, where I commenced this letter. This is a town of some twenty thousand people, strongly antichristian, who gave us many scowls as we passed through the town. This being noted as a hard place, we had some eight or ten soldiers from the barracks added to our guard force for the night.

The people here manufacture large quantities of olive soap, which they brought to our tents for sale, also tobacco pouches made of goat and sheep skins. We went into a Samaritan church, and saw the priest, and bought some of his photographs. He showed us the five books of Moses written on parchment that was thirty-five hundred years old. Nablous is famous for its great number of springs coming out of Mount Gerizim, which are used along down the valley for irrigation, producing beautiful fields and gardens. These springs are refreshing to a traveller in this country, as there is a terrible dearth of that article through Palestine.

Friday, the 26th, we were on the march bright and early, passing down the valley some two miles over a fine road which leads to Jaffa. But we are bound for Nazareth. So we turn to the right into a bridle-path, and begin to climb; and, when you are near the top of this elevation, cast your eye to the south, looking across the valley we have just left to the hill the other side, and you will get the grandest view in Palestine. The side of the mountain is somewhat free from stone, and seems to be terraced up the beautiful slopes with straight, conical, and crescent terraces, covered with a rich verdure, filled with the flowers of the land.

We pass over this mountain, and as we commence to descend the other side, we see across the valley the historical town of Samaria, standing upon a high elevation. We descend into the valley, and climb up into one of the oldest and most degraded-looking towns we have been called upon to pass through. We saw the pool of Samaria where Ahab's chariot was washed. Ahab was slain in his chariot in battle and taken to this place. Here he had his winter residence with his ivory palace. We saw some of the foundation and columns, which is all that is left of it. We saw some of the columns of the colonnade that extended from the city gate to the palace, some three thousand feet. We leave this town, once so splendid, feeling that sin and misery have done their perfect work. The rest of the day we are passing through wheat fields and one of the largest olive orchards in Palestine, and at five o'clock reach Jenin where we tent for the night.

Jenin is on the border of the wonderful valley of Esdraelon. This town is modern, but is said to be the place where Christ healed the ten lepers. Here we saw some palm-trees which made us think of Egypt. It was a question whether they were strayed or stolen; but they looked thrifty, and we decided that the breezes from the valley of Esdraelon had been fanning them. This valley is different from the Jordan, being rich and fertile; and, unlike the prairies of the West, it has many conical hills and even mountains scattered over its broad acres. And, as in David's and Solomon's time, Jerusalem and Mount Zion were the joy of the whole earth in a spiritual sense, so, it seems to me, the valley of Esdraelon must have been the joy in a temporal view. It seems to be the great granary of Palestine.

Saturday morning, the 27th, the sun rose clear and bright, and we expected a scorching day across the valley, which takes nearly all day; but the Lord sent the clouds to cover us as he did the children of Israel, and we had the most satisfactory day of the week. One hour from Jenin we reached Jezreel, standing upon a high elevation. Here was Ahab's summer residence, here also was Naboth's vineyard. We rode upon this elevation, left our saddles, and looked over the town, which now consists mostly of mud huts, save the old stone palace and the window where Jezebel came down, and the dogs devoured her; and I have the impression that they have kept in Palestine the same breed of dogs ever since, for we find here the meanest dogs in the world. They seem to delight in barking nights, keeping poor mortals awake. If some one could get at them with stones and knock the bark off of them, it would be a blessing to every one.

Now, if you will stand by me on this elevation with your face northward, looking down on the plain at your right, you will see the fountain of Gideon. In front of you is where the Midianite forces were gathered when Gideon routed them with his hundred men. Now look across the valley some three miles to another mountain elevation, which is Little Hermon. At the base is the town of Shunem, where the woman had the prophet's chamber, where Elisha raised the boy to life. Now cast your eye to the left some ten miles distant, and you see Mount Carmel. To this mount the servant ran for Elisha; and the prophet asked, "Is it well with the child?"

We mount our horses, and descend from Jezreel into the valley, and soon are at the town of Shunem. Going through the town, we turn to the left, winding our way around the base of this elevation, reaching the other side, where we find the town of Nain, where Christ raised the widow's son. Here we find our luncheon-tent, and remain here some two hours.

About two miles north of us is Mount Tabor, where, it has been claimed, the transfiguration took place. We are about two hours' ride from Nazareth. Leaving at 2.30, we soon finish crossing the valley of Esdraelon, and go up a steep elevation with bad roads. We make our way gradually, rising several hundred feet above the plain. We then make a little descent into a valley almost surrounded by hills, and find the beautiful little town of Nazareth. You will call it a place of retirement. Here is a little valley with hills surrounding it, from fifty to one hundred feet high. At first sight, you will say the plateau of land is round; but on close examination you will decide the length is nearly twice the width, which, I should say, is less than a half-mile across. The buildings are not on this plain, but are in crescent form at the base of the hills.

At the upper part of the valley the plain is used as a common and for gardens. We are tented on the common of some twenty-five acres, carpeted with green grass and dotted with flowers, spending the Sabbath in quiet. Dr. Dunning preached to us to-day as we gathered in front of our dining-tent, taking for his subject, largely, the human side of the life of Christ, and made it very interesting. Nowhere could such a sermon be made so impressive as here, where Christ's childhood days were spent. We have visited the workshop of Joseph and the home of Mary, the church of annunciation, where the angel appeared to Mary the virgin, the fountain, the synagogue where Christ taught; and we have been through the bazaars and many of the straight and narrow streets.

Nazareth, unlike many towns in this region, is strongly Christian, — three thousand nine hundred Christian and nineteen hundred of other classes, — not a Jew lives here, — a much better class of people than we usually meet, and many neat and pretty children, fine-looking women coming to Mary's fountain and filling their water-jars, that hold from one to two pails. We found these jars to be heavy, and put one of them upon Mrs. Dunning's head. There were many of these women at the fountain, and they seemed to enjoy the interview we had with them; and we were interested to see them walk off with the jar on their heads with such indifference.

We came into Nazareth from the south over a rough road, and shall go north-east Monday to Tiberias, expecting a much better road.

MONDAY, the 29th.

Our ride to Tiberias is a long one. Therefore, we are called at five o'clock, and are in the saddle at six, wending our way up the hill out of Nazareth, taking with regret a farewell look at the prettiest town we have seen yet, since we placed our feet in the land of Palestine. The Jews thought no good thing could come out of this little town among the mountains; but the stone that was cut out of the mountain here is filling the whole earth, and there seems to be a hallowed sacredness as we tread the same streets that were trodden by Him who came to bless all mankind.

One hour takes us over the hill down into a beautiful valley; and at one side of the valley, nestled upon the brow of the hill, stands the little village of Cana. In front and around it are spread out the groves of olives, figs, and pomegranate trees, making a beautiful picture. At the edge of the town is a copious spring, where they water their flocks, and the maidens come with their water-jars.

We went into the town, and at the church we saw the old stone water-pots that were used at the wedding; and, certainly, they looked old enough to have been used in Noah's ark.

From Cana we passed on through a beautiful country, valleys, and elevations, where we could canter our horses at pleasure. We passed the home of Jonah, and about ten o'clock came to the Mount of Beatitudes. The day was hot; but old snow-capped Hermon, towering up nine thousand feet, seemingly a short distance to our left, seemed to nod his head to us, saying, "Keep cool."

The place where it is supposed Christ preached his wonderful sermon is a small, conical hill, some fifty feet high, with the ground gradually sloping from it, and is beautiful to look upon. Whether this is the place or some other elevation near here makes but little difference. We have the sermon, rich in thought,— principles laid down, that are, for the healing of the nations; and it seems as though Nature in her beauty in this locality responded to those teachings, and said, "Amen," for no artist with pencil and brush, tapestry and Persian art added, could attract the eye of the lovers of the beautiful as the hills, vales, and dales about the Mount of Beatitudes. The hills here are different from those about Jerusalem. They have lost their granite and limestone ribs, and this is a section of country that would attract a Vermont farmer.

We pass on from this point, and sight the Sea of Galilee down deep in the valley, with its peaceful waters. We wend our way down a steep hill, and soon are at the little seaport town of Tiberias. Passing through the village down the shore half a mile, we find our lunch-tent. Just below it is the hot sulphur spring, with bathing-houses; and they are patronized by many people. We spend some time on the shore, gathering pebbles and shells. We can see the whole length of the sea, thirteen miles; and it averages six miles wide. Yet you would not think it to be half that distance.

Few places in Palestine have more historical interest connected with the three years' labor of the Saviour than the Sea of Galilee. We wondered where he fed the multitude, where he launched out in a boat and taught the people, at what point was he when he stilled the waters, where did he order the disciples to cast the net on the other side of the boat, etc. We now are near the south end of the lake, which runs north and south. Here we take four sail and row boats going north. When we start, the waters are smooth as glass, and our oarsmen, four of them to each boat, use the oars; but before we had been on the water half an hour the wind seemed to come down upon us, and they spread their sails, and we sped through the troubled waters rapidly. It was wonderful how quickly the waters were troubled. At the head of the lake we visit the old site of Capernaum. About all there is left is the location, and few ruins, except a new building occupied by the monks.

From this spot we sail west, passing the old town of Bethsaida, the home of the fishermen that Christ called to be his disciples, landing at the plains of Chinnereth, where we camp for the night. We were three hours on the water, and enjoyed it much. The river Jordan enters the Sea of Galilee at the north end, leaving it at the south end, going on its way sixty miles to the Dead Sea. When we reached our tents, our day's work was done, being full of interest all the way from Nazareth to the sea.

Tuesday morning we started north up over the mountain. Found a rough country. We let our horses have the bit and bridle, and they took us over places we hope never to pass again. Yesterday we were going to send for our Vermont farmer friend, as we had found the garden of the world; but to-day we are ready to say "stick to Vermont." After three hours' ride we seemed to be on the top of the mountain, and could look south and see the Sea of Galilee, look north and see the waters of Merom, where we are tenting to-night. Our tents form a circle; and in the circle we have a bonfire, and are being entertained by about fifty Bedouins, singing and dancing and practising with the broadsword. We had our lunch to-day some three miles south of this place, where there was a large spring coming out of the mountain. Fine water for this country, and enough of it to run a grist mill of some four run of stones; but the grain feeds into the mill about as fast as a good smart Vermont hen would pick it up, and was the crudest mill mortal man ever set eyes upon.

After leaving the Sea of Galilee and crossing the mountain, we came into the Jordan valley, but skirted along its edge near the mountain, and found many springs coming out of the mountains, sending their streams of pure water out into that historic river, the Jordan. We are now travelling in the region of Naphtali. Up the valley Joshua swept with his army when he took the land of Canaan.

BEDOUINS WITH THEIR HARPS.

The Jordan valley here is much more fertile than we found it at Jericho, and is almost wholly occupied by the Bedouins. They live in tents unlike any other tent you will have the privilege of looking upon. They have cloth made out of goat's hair, black, which is set up on sticks, the highest in the centre being long and narrow, raised five or six feet from the ground. Around the edges they fit up bamboo or anything they can get. I have counted seventy of these tents in a cluster. It makes a black-looking village. The tents are black, the skin of the people the same color, the character as black as you please. They till the soil but very little. They have their cattle, living on milk and beef, with some poultry and eggs, and roam from place to place as herdsmen. The cattle here in Palestine are mostly small black cattle; when grown, about the size of our yearlings.

But I see in this valley the Bedouins have some of the Egyptian breed of cattle. They are large, coarse, and homely. I think they would smile to see our Vermont Durhams.

VI.

WEDNESDAY, May 1.

We have been travelling most of the day in the valley. Yesterday we were going north on the west side: to-day, about 10 A.M., we head our horses eastward, crossing to the other side of the plain. We went over an old arched stone bridge, which took us across one of the largest tributaries of the Jordan River, and were soon at the Hill of Dan, where we took our lunch under two large live-oak trees, measuring sixteen and nineteen feet in circumference. The boughs of one of them spread ninety feet. So you see we had plenty of room for forty people.

Just east of these trees lie the ruins of Dan. Here was where Jeroboam set up the golden calf to accommodate the people, when he established himself at Bethel. Here we went into another gristmill, two hundred years old. They could grind one bushel an hour in each run of stones.

When leaving this place, we go up on to some high table land, sparsely covered with live oaks and trees of a similar character, which we enjoyed, as we had seen nothing of the kind for many days.

After a short ride we came to a valley where is located the town of Banias, the former Cæsarea Philippi, where we spend the night. Here is the head of the Jordan River. One of the spurs of Mount Hermon came down to this place, ending with a perpendicular ledge. From under this ledge came out a great flow of water, and it is really the beginning of that historic river, and is about the size of the Black River at Springfield, but receives many tributaries as it flows on. Cæsarea Philippi was built by Philip the Tetrarch, and was somewhat a Roman town. It is thought to resemble Tivoli, and the old ruin signifies that once it was a flourishing place. This was the furthest point north the Saviour ever went, and that for only once; and it is supposed while here he went with Peter and John on to one of the spurs of Mount Hermon, and was transfigured before them. He was baptized in the waters of the Jordan. At its source he was transfigured. He calmed its waters as it passed through the Sea of Galilee. He called most of his disciples from its locality, and the Jordan flows on in rich, historic memories.

When we left Banias, we entered the land of Syria, and were informed that our luncheon-tent would be on the mountains, five thousand feet above the sea. Therefore, we began to climb. In some three hours we halted at quite a good-sized town, inhabited by the Druses. This is the class of people that slaughtered so many Christians in 1860. Many of the men, women, and children, came out to see us, and to sell their wares and trinkets. The men were all armed with dirk-knives, and showed us how to use them. Some of them use one in each hand with great dexterity. We should have been satisfied to have known how they didn't use them. The sheik of the town was there, and he brought out a piece of bread, divided it in two parts with our manager, and they ate it together. That was a token of peace; and we mounted our horses, and passed on to where we found our luncheon-tent. For the last few hours the snow-capped peaks of Mount Hermon were close to our left. Around them were the lower peaks and spurs. Hermon looked like a white-bearded old fellow with his children settled all about him, located for all time, if not eternity.

The day proved to be one of the worst of our experience. It was what I should call intermittent.

First the sun would shine, then it would rain, and, to make it poetical, we would next have sunshine, then a snow-squall, the wind blowing almost a gale; but, as luck would have it, it was at our backs. Parties have had to turn back and wait for better weather before going over the mountain; but we kept in the saddle until after five o'clock, at which time we were nearly over the mountain, and tented for the night at the little town of Henah. But the wind and storm still continued. Our tents fluttered and trembled, but the guy ropes were thoroughly fastened and attended to through the night; and everything was kept intact until the next morning, when we went on our way rejoicing.

Coming over the mountain, we had three exhibits of the most gorgeous rainbow mortal man ever beheld,—one end resting on the plain below us, the other on the mountain. The question was, was such an exhibit common to Syria or was it expressly for the Congregational party.

After leaving Henah, our objective point was Damascus, which we expected to reach about 4 P.M. We crossed in the forenoon the waters of Pharpar, and about eleven o'clock reached the Damascus plains. What we have seen of Syria so far is anything but flattering. The soil is very poor, and strewn in many places with lava, rock, and wheat headed out when from six to twelve inches high. It is under the Turkish government; and the people are taxed to death, as they are in the whole empire.

We have been travelling over the main road from Jerusalem to Damascus; and it was somewhere near

Damascus that Saul of Tarsus was converted, or at least found out that it was hard to kick against the pricks.

As you come down on to the plains, you are near the west side; and you have at your left the Anti-Lebanon Mountains, which form a beautiful background to the plain which stretches far to the east, with lesser hills and mountains beyond. Near the head of this valley your eye beholds a beautiful grove, variegated, stretching from the Anti-Lebanon Mountains across the head of the plains for miles. Above the trees you will see a great number of white towers and minarets, and you will decide that you are soon to be in that city where the great apostle Paul dated his conversion.

Our head dragoman had a little pride left, even after being with us so many days; and, as we were a larger party than he usually has the privilege of conducting, he wished to take us into the city in good order. So we were commanded to stop at the gate of the city until we were all together, then rode two abreast, with the dragoman at the head.

Going into Damascus is like going into the maze at Monterey, in California. The road, which is fair in width, is lined each side with walls built of clay and small stones mixed together, which are from four to ten feet high; and you are all the time turning angles. Where these walls are not so high but what you can look over them, you will see gardens and groves. Here you find the silver-leaf poplar growing, which is used for building. Then it is a forest of fruit-trees, olives, walnut, fig, etc. Nothing seemngly grown in Palestine but what you will find here in Damascus. It is said that Mohammed, when he stood upon the mountain, at the head of the city, and looked upon it, exclaimed, "There is but one paradise, and that is Damascus." The city has over two hundred thousand inhabitants and some two hundred mosques. It is an old city, and has had terrible conflicts. Even as late as 1860 there were six thousand Christians murdered here.

David conquered the place after a bloody war, as it was allied with his enemy, the king of Zobah. (See 2 Samuel viii. 5, 6.) During the reign of Solomon an adventurer by the name of Rezin made himself king. At one time the Romans had control, and you can see to-day the old Roman arch and gate.

We have visited the houses of Ananias and Judas, that are connected with Paul's history, also the place where he was let down in a basket.

The city has a wonderful water supply, the river Abana running through it. From this stream, water is taken in all directions. The main part of the stream is carried through the city in a canal, which is some sixty feet wide, and runs swiftly. The water has a pearly appearance.

We have, in my opinion, reached the climax on dogs here in Damascus. We find it is against the law to kill a dog; and they are lying about the streets, on the sidewalks, or anywhere they choose, appearing sleepy, as if they had been up all night. You can count from ten to twenty anywhere you may happen to be.

There are many rich men here who have fine residences. Some of our party visited one of these places, where one room cost fifty thousand dollars.

VEILED WOMEN.

VII.

DAMASCUS, May 2, 1895.

We are stopping at the Grand Hotel, Besraoui; and we find it first-class. When we alighted from our horses in front of the hotel, two large iron doors, some fifteen feet high, swung open. In one of these doors is the needle eye; that is, a small door in one of the large doors, that can be used when the large doors are closed, although a short person has to stoop to pass through. We enter a hall or vestibule. At your right is the office, at your left the parlor. In front is a court some fifty feet square, paved with marble, large fountain in the centre, lemon-trees growing, full of fruit. Before stepping into this court, you can turn to the right or left, going up stairs leading on to balconies that are built round on three sides of the court. From these balconies you open the doors into your rooms. We are located on the first floor, having a very pleasant room.

We remain here until Tuesday, the 7th, then finish our camping tour to Beyrout.

You will remember that Paul went to the street called Straight, to the house of Judas, and Ananias was sent for, etc. This street referred to was a wonderful street, although it was not straight, but was the nearest to the line and plummet of any street in Damascus; for, if you wish to get angles and curves to perfection, then come to this city. The street called Straight in Paul's day was ninety feet wide, and was the great market-place.

Here come the caravans from Persia,— a hundred camels at once, loaded with merchandise. Since that time buildings have been put through the centre of the street, making two streets out of one, and greatly increasing the number of bazaars; and the camels stop outside the city.

While Damascus has shade-trees and many fine things, yet a large part of it is filthy; and our party think they prefer Cairo. The people in Cairo are not as foreign as they are in Damascus. The people here use mostly goats' milk. We see droves of them coming into the city to be milked, but no cows. The churning of milk or cream through Palestine and Syria is done in goat-skins, which are sewed up, then the milk put inside and shaken.

When we were passing through the Bedouin country, the women and children would come out with the dirtiest, crudest-looking receptacles, with milk and buttermilk to sell; but I think our party must have been out of funds, for I did not see them purchase any of the tempting nectar. We have also been interested in the way the people do their washing. They go to the brook and wash the clothes on a flat rock, sometimes using another flat stone to pound and rub them with. The people and their ways are extremely queer to us, but I presume we are as much of a curiosity to them.

We found here in Damascus to-day the father of lemons. It measured the smallest way round thirteen and one-half inches, the other way seventeen inches. We of course took the largest one in the pile to try our tape-line on.

They keep six thousand soldiers here to look after the peace of the city. Safety would call for more rather than less.

The last day of our stay here our party took a carriage ride through and around Damascus, and drove on to the hill near the mountain where Mohammed stood when he admired the city so much; and we could but exclaim, "Beautiful!" But as we had been through its dusty streets, and seen its miserable houses, we decided it was one of those places where distance lends enchantment. The sweeping waters of the Abana pass close by our hotel.

Tuesday morning, the 7th, we were on our horses, and bade good-by to Damascus, directing our course up the beautiful Abana, and soon were in a narrow valley between the high mountains, and our eyes were drinking in the finest scenery in the world. The road was fine, being the main road to Beyrout.

After an hour's ride we turned to the right, and took to the mountains, for Baalbec was our objective point; and we found ourselves going over the Anti-Libanus Mountain, which gave us some grand scenery. We could at times look down thousands of feet into the valley of green trees, and see the Abana River and the new railroad that is being built, meandering their way down to the great city of Damascus. We scale the mountain, and descend into a valley, where we find one of the tributaries of the Abana boiling up from under large rocks at the base of the mountain; and we wonder and admire to see the great quantities of pure water rushing away from this fountain, going on its errand of mercy to the arid plains below. Here was a beautiful grove cooled by the rivers of water; and our dragoman had spread our lunch table in the cooling shade, where we spent two enjoyable hours. As a little episode, one of our horses broke down one of the trees in the grove. Very soon a middle-aged woman appeared, gesticulating and jabbering with all her powers, her eyes flashing. I thought at first we were to be driven off the grounds. Evidently, she believed in woman's rights; and I rather admired her spunk, but was disgusted to see how easily she was bought up. Our head dragoman went and picked up a few pieces of bread we had left at lunch, and gave to her; and she went off, smiling and happy as a clam in high water.

After two hours' ride we reached the town of Suk, where we camped for the night. Here the mountains are near to us, rising almost perpendicular more than one thousand feet. Upon the top of one of these mountains you will see a tomb, a building quite conspicuous. Tradition says it is the tomb of Abel.

Our tents are close by the new railroad they are building from Damascus to Beyrout. We examined it, and found that they were laying the rails on iron ties. They are made like a trough, and bolted firmly to these iron sleepers.

Wednesday morning we commence our journey, going through the grandest scenery we have seen this side of the Atlantic. In half an hour we halt, and look over the sections of the old Roman road. Another half-hour brings us into a broad, fertile valley, should call it the Esdraelon of Syria.

Since we left Damascus we have been crossing the Anti-Lebanon Mountains, sometimes in the valleys, then again on the mountains, most of the time old snow-capped Hermon plain in view. 5 P.M. finds us tented at the town of Yafufeh.

Thursday morning, the 9th, we are off for Baalbec, having a ride of four hours, arriving at 10 A.M. Here we spend the rest of the day, as there is much of interest to look over. There might be a book written confined to Baalbec, or Heliopolis, its ancient name, the former meaning God of the Valley, the latter City of the Sun. But time will only permit me to give you a few outlines, and advise you, if ever in Syria, not to fail to see the most wonderful ruins in the world. You will be amazed by both quantity and quality of the ruins, covering acres of ground. In its walls are stones for you to examine, sixty-three feet long, thirteen feet in breadth and width, that weigh twelve hundred tons, some of them twenty feet from the ground. How to place such a stone in position would be a hard problem for the stone-masons of the nineteenth century to solve. In wandering through these, you are continually reminded that once, notwithstanding its vastness, it must have been beautiful. The beautiful stucco-work of to-day might well be traced back to the carving in stone seen in these ruins. It is somewhat of a mystery who commenced these temples. Some suppose it to have been Solomon. It must have been a man of great resources.

Baalbec has now five thousand inhabitants, many Christians among them, and a much better class of people than the average in Syria. It was at one time a commercial centre. It is beautiful for situation, is near the base of the Anti-Lebanon Mountains, near the head of the plain or valley Bekaa, or the old name Cœle-Syria, and divides Anti-Lebanon from Lebanon. There is a large spring coming out of the mountain about a mile above the town, which forms quite a river of pure water that flows through the city; and the plain below this covers the valley about Baalbec with beautiful groves and great variety of trees, both useful and ornamental. Up to this fountain, named Rosel Ain, from the town, is a charming drive, the avenue lined each side with willows nourished by the stream of water that follows the avenue. At the west you see the Lebanon Mountain; and a short ride will take you to the cedar groves, the pride of this historic elevation. Those forests, we understand, have been greatly reduced since Solomon's time. You will remember that Hiram furnished Solomon with great quantities of this timber when he built the temple. Solomon sent eighty thousand men to perform the work. This would open the eyes even of a Maine or Michigan man, to see such a logging camp. This was used in Solomon's palaces, as well as the temple. Herod also drew upon the forest. In history wars and rumors of wars have hovered around Baalbec; and it has suffered in that way, as have all important centres in this country. At one time one of the temples was turned into a fortress.

Sun-worship was the leading idolatry, and every year they sacrificed human beings. At a later day

Constantine came in, and for a while established Christian worship. The destruction of these temples has mostly been by earthquakes,— granite columns, from four to six feet through, broken in pieces, piled up in heaps, the wall in many places shaken down.

Friday morning, the 10th, we are on the east side of the Cœle-Syria valley; and in leaving this place, Baalbec, we take a carriage road, which is quite a treat to us. Following this road, we cross to the west side of the plain, then, turning southward, we ride all day down this beautiful valley, and at night are camped near Shatora. At this place we strike the diligence road from Damascus to Beyrout. This road, seventy miles in length, was built by a French company, and crosses over Mount Lebanon. It must have been expensive; but they apply the toll to it, so they receive about twenty per cent. on their investment. The road is a fine one, and the engineering over the mountain made me think of the railroad over the Rocky Mountains.

SATURDAY, the 11th.

To-day we finish our camping tour. We are to cross over Mount Lebanon, reaching Beyrout, thirty-five miles distant. So at six o'clock we are in the saddle, and soon begin to climb the mountain, looking back down into the valley and across to Anti-Lebanon; and in the distance beyond is old snow-capped Hermon. This old fellow has had his eye on us most of the time for the last ten days; but up we climb until about eleven o'clock, and find ourselves on top of Mount Lebanon, and at twelve stop for lunch at the town of Kahnel Sheik. You will remember that our first lunch was at Bethel; and here at this place we say Amen, and bid good-by to our tents.

From this point you can see the blue Mediterranean; and upon an elevation lies the city of Beyrout, dipping her feet down into the sea. This side of the city, and at the foot of the mountain, is a valley sweeping around the city, covered with trees, dotted with white cottages, forming the suburbs of the city, the sleeping place for the busy crowd that spend the day-time near the sea. We can look down into many ravines, see many villages tucked away in retirement, and at other places they have hung them up on the mountains, and we wonder how in the world the people ever reach their homes; but, where there is a will, there is a way.

The day has been one of grand scenery; and, after halting an hour, we move on down the mountain, and when within some four miles of the city we meet a very pleasant surprise. It seems the people of the American college here in Beyrout had been watching us, and were ready to give us a welcome. In the distance we saw a troop of men coming on fine horses. This cavalcade proved to be President Bliss, who was born in Georgia, Vt., with his professors, also Mr. Gibson, the American consul. President Bliss has a personal acquaintance with some of our party, and we were very pleasantly escorted into Beyrout.

The last few days we have been among the mulberry-trees, and one of the products of this country is silk. In Damascus there are three thousand hand looms weaving this article, also great quantities produced here in Beyrout. So, young ladies, if you admire silk dresses, here is the place to come.

Over the road between here and Damascus, which I have referred to, they run a vehicle each way every day, called a diligence. It is somewhat different from a Concord coach. It seats twelve persons, all inside, except the man that holds the ribbons. They start early in the morning, reaching their destination at 5 P.M., covering the seventy miles in that time. Six horses is the number used, driving three abreast; and they have a fresh relay every six miles.

We spend eight days here in Beyrout, and then sail for Athens, making several calls along the coast.

Will give you more about Beyrout and beyond here in my next letter.

VIII.

BEYROUT, May 16.

You have been following us in our camping tour, and perhaps you would like to take a glimpse of our caravan as we are camping and also on the move. We have some sixteen tents, each tent accommodating two persons, also dining and cooking tents. The members of the party from Springfield have a tent by themselves. It is fifteen feet in diameter, being round, the sides six feet high, with a conical top, and tent pole in the centre reaching up fifteen feet. The canopy top projects over the sides some twelve inches, making a neat finish, and is held out by guy ropes. The outside is striped excepting the top, which is white. The inside is covered with beautiful needlework, squares, diamond-shaped pieces, flowers, etc., handsome as tapestry. The ground is our floor, but is covered with carpets. We have two beds with iron frames, table, two wash-bowls, two pitchers, brass candlestick with candle, chairs, etc.

Around the tent pole, up some six feet, is buckled a strap with hooks for hanging clothes. We sleep sound, and come out fresh in the morning. There may be a few bugs, spiders, or fleas that will want to get into bed with you before morning; but that, you know, is nothing, when you are on a picnic.

We found out after we were on the way from Jerusalem that we had one hundred and five horses, mules, and donkeys, and forty-eight men, dragomen, muleteers, and helpers to move us. We have two large copper bells, large enough to call people to church, that are put on the leading mules of our baggage train. These they ring in the morning at 5.30 o'clock to call us to rise and prepare for breakfast, which is ready at six. Before you leave your tent, you must pack your trunk and valises; and while at breakfast these articles will be taken out and packed in large rubber-lined bags, ready to strap on the mules.

We have for breakfast tea, coffee, good bread, omelets or fried eggs, and mutton chops. When you come out of the dining tent, you will find nearly all of the tents down and packed. Before we are called in the morning, men start with our lunch-tent and eatables, which consist of bread, cold chicken, beef, and mutton, cold boiled eggs, raisins, nuts and oranges. We are in the saddle at 6.30, and proceed, led by dragomen, of which we have three, one of these being always at the rear to look after the stragglers and lazy ones. Then there are several helpers. So if a lady's saddle should turn or girt break, or any other trouble occur, there is always some one at hand to see that it is righted. Our three dragomen all speak English, and are fine fellows. Our managers, Mr. Vicker, an Englishman, and Mr. Voight, a German, are also with the party.

About noon or before we spy our lunch-tent, usually in some grove or by some good spring. Our horses are turned over to the helpers, who have their grain and feed-bags with them; and we go to our lunch, and usually before we are through we hear those big bells, and, looking out, will see our baggage train passing. This train makes no stop after it starts in the morning until it reaches our next tenting place. We wait one and one-half hours after this train passes before we begin our afternoon journey. We have four ladies that did not dare risk horseback riding so long a journey, so hired palanquins. This is a narrow wagon body with a wooden top, with strips of wood on each side running out before and behind, forming shafts for the mules, which have on a large pillion saddle; and these shafts are attached to that. A man on a donkey leads the front mule, and a man behind brings up the rear, thus taking two men, two mules, and a donkey to run one of these vehicles. They charge five dollars per day for them. They have proved rather troublesome things over some of the rough places we have travelled. They usually start these vehicles on ahead, as they do not go as fast as the horses like to travel.

About four or five o'clock we usually spy our white city in some grove or by some spring, which is always a delight. The tents are all numbered, and each one knows his number. When we alight, the first thing is to find our tent with beds all made up, baggage intact, etc. In a few minutes the bell rings for tea, which with crackers they furnish us on arrival. Being thirsty, about three cups of weak tea with as many crackers as you please are very refreshing. Then you can rest in your tent or visit among your neighbors. The latter is the most popular thing to do. At seven the bell rings for dinner. First course, hot soup, then follow usually three courses of meat and fish, closing up with some fancy dish and raisins, nuts, and oranges. Our head cook is paid four dollars per day, and we think he is worth it. When you retire, you can have your hot-water bags filled if you wish; and I notice a good many of them skipping around among the tents, as we get cool nights in this country.

Before starting on this tour, we had our doubts on the matter; but the idea of seeing so much of interest nerved us to the battle. But we can now say that we have enjoyed it, and come out hale and hearty. Some of us have become so attached to our horses that we almost want to take them home with us.

IX.

BEYROUT, May 17, 1895.

April 15 we landed on the sultan's territory, and have been and are still under Turkish rule. We expect to leave the 19th for Athens, making several stops at important places along the coast.

Turkey is under the iron hand of Mohammedanism,' being filled with Mohammedans, Mussulmans, Bedouins, etc. There are only a few places where Christianity gets much of a foothold. Beyrout is one of them; but the great principle for the healing of the nations gains ground hereabout as the doctor said about his patient,—"improved wonderfully, but very slowly."

We talked with the missionaries at Damascus. They said, if one of the natives should change his religion from Mohammedanism to Christianity, his life would not be worth a penny. The only thing he could do would be to flee the country. Therefore, direct mission work is virtually cut off; and all they can do is to work among the children, educating them and instilling into their minds the principles of freedom.

There was an English lady at work there who was converted at the age of twenty, a lady of culture and wealth, who has a brother in Parliament. After her conversion she felt that she must give her all to the mission work. She commenced her work in Damascus, and has already educated six hundred children, and is still at the good work,— a consecrated life.

I believe the time is coming when Turkey will wheel into line, and the principle that is grinding the people to the earth will give way to those principles that elevate humanity. The American college here is doing a good work. This college was endowed largely with American capital. They have nearly two hundred and fifty students. The president and professors are having a strong influence on Beyrout, which is a growing city. When President Bliss came here thirty or more years ago, there were forty thousand people here. Now there are over one hundred thousand, and it is unquestionably the brightest town in Syria.

Tuesday, the 13th, our party took carriages, and drove to Dog River, up the bay, seven and one-half miles. From this river comes the water supply for the city. On our way we pass the old stone chapel where, it is said, Saint George had the tussle with the dragon. The river is named from what tradition says: that there was a stone dog out in the sea, at the mouth of this river, that used to bark at the approach of an enemy. Sensible dog, surely. Another tradition, and a more sensible one, is that there was a peculiar-shaped rock on the cliff by the sea, that, when the wind blew hard, made a howling noise, like a dog. However, aside from all the dog business, it is a place of much interest.

The new road that has been lately built up the bay has a beautiful stone bridge across this river near its mouth as it empties into the sea. The Lebanon Mountains at this point almost reach the blue waters of the Mediterranean; and just before you reach the bridge, at your right, you will notice the old Roman road, winding its way up the mountain. Here at the commencement of this road is much of historical interest.

Many tablets of large size are cut in the rocks of the mountain. The first one you notice speaks of the history of Napoleon, and is the latest one, being carved in 1860. This famous general came out to fight the Turks, and one of his brave generals fell here. There are several tablets of the Pharaohs, also one that is supposed to have been placed there by Sennacherib, some seven hundred years before Christ. You will remember that he lay siege to Jerusalem, and was at Samaria, and had cut off all supplies, so there was a terrible famine, when Elijah prophesied that in so many hours bread would be sold in the gates of Samaria, etc. The angel of the Lord caused Sennacherib's army to hear the approaching enemy in great numbers, and fled in wild confusion; and the lepers were the first ones to enter the camp and find plenty of food.

This old Roman road was, no doubt, the one he took his army over; and the tablet might have been placed here in memory of that event. As we climbed up over this road, we thought of Mark Twain's saying, that you could tell where these Roman roads were by finding the places where there were the most stones. Another of Mark's neat sayings has been buzzing in our ears the last three weeks,— that people here know nothing about distances in miles. You ask them how far any place is, they always say so many minutes or hours.

Mark went into a tailor shop to get a pair of trousers, and he told the man he wanted them so many seconds around the waist and so many minutes down the leg. No doubt the tailor knew just what he wanted.

Our ride to Dog River, the entire seven and one-half miles, was through gardens and mulberry orchards. The trunks of the trees are allowed to grow about seven feet tall, then they throw out shoots, in number anywhere from fifteen to thirty on a tree, and are allowed to grow to the length of some five feet. This growth is obtained in a few weeks, and the shoots are full of tender leaves, which are cut off and fed to the worms; and other sprouts grow in their places.

They raise a sort of bamboo or cane here that grows six or eight feet high. The natives cut this, and build booths in the orchard, setting it up on end, and throwing a covering over the top. Inside they build shelves on which you can find the silk-worm. They throw over them these green mulberry leaves, and the ravenous fellows devour them. They are fed three times during the day and twice in the night. They appear to be very religious in their habits. They fast every week, eating some five days, then fasting two days. In forty days they are through with this world's goods, and commence to make goods for other people, forming the cocoons from which the beautiful silks are made that all admire.

As you pass along the streets of Beyrout, about every third place you look into you will see the hand loom running, weaving silk for market. One occupation we have found here in Beyrout that we have not seen anywhere else; that is, fortune-telling. You will see old duffers sitting on the sidewalk, with a cloth some twenty inches square, covered with fine sand; and beside them an ink-horn, pen, and paper. They look a person over, and with three fingers dot the sand all over, and will then write out your future history. But the future of the Congregationalist party is unfolding as fast as we care to know it. Therefore, we leave these old Arabs alone in their glory.

Many of the streets here are lined with beautiful trees. The pride of China, looking much like the pepper-tree of California, is very abundant. It has a heavier foliage, and many would prefer it to the pepper-tree. Then we find another tree they call the macher, and one has to see it in order to know its beauty. It is large, some twenty-five feet high, and literally covered from top to bottom with a blue or purple flower ; and you will never pass one without admiration.

Wednesday, the 15th, we were all invited to a reception at the college from 3 to 7 P.M. Being one and one-half miles away, carriages took us there, and came for us at 7 P.M. The college buildings are located on high ground away from the business part of the city, close to the blue sea, so near seemingly that you could throw a stone into its waters. They were hoping to give us a chance to view and admire one of their beautiful sunsets; but, unfortunately, it was cloudy. The Lebanon Mountains with their variegated green, and the blue waters of the Mediterranean, with the expiring rays of day mingled with the shadows of coming night, form a picture that will satisfy the eye of all lovers of the beautiful.

We were shown through the college buildings, and were very much interested. The museum was fine. They have a fine chapel, given by Mr. Monroe, of New York, seating one thousand people. William E. Dodge in his day did much for this institution. His sons are still interested. They have a fine astronomical observatory, with fine telescope with twelve-inch glass, manufactured by Warren & Swazey, of Cleveland, Ohio, at a cost of over eight thousand dollars.

At five o'clock we went to the spread in large rooms, suitable for the occasion. Tea, coffee, and lemonade, and such biscuits and cake we have not looked upon or tasted since we left America. It was like attending a church sociable. They have connected with this college a medical department with a four years' course of study, turning out thorough physicians that have been successful in their vocation.

We found the president and professors, with their wives, daughters, and sons, remarkably cordial and social; and we came away feeling indebted to them for a royal good time, which we placed in the book of our remembrance, and it will be one of the pleasantest episodes of the Congregationalist tour.

This American mission, now Presbyterian, has been at work in Syria since 1821. We have also visited the girls' school, publishing house, and church connected with this mission. Many eminent and scientific men have been connected with this work, such as Eli Smith, Van Dyck, Thompson, and others. They have a beautiful Sunday-school chapel, built on the spot where Van Dyck translated the first Arabic Bible. This chapel has its class-rooms with sliding glass doors, and would do credit to any American city. In the church they have service every Sunday at nine o'clock in English, and at eleven o'clock in Arabic. We attended the English service. They have a fine organ, excellent choir, having a fine soprano singer. The publishing house is doing a good business, turning out many Bibles in Arabic and publishing a paper. But the government annoys them in this matter. Nothing can be printed in this line without first being sent to the censor. If there is anything he does not like, he draws his pen through it; and that ends the matter. The government is very jealous, and the mails are watched closely. It is hard to get a newspaper in or out of Turkey. Every telegram is examined by some government official. No cipher telegrams can be sent from this country. However, this printing establishment has pluck and forbearance, and are employing over fifty hands, doing some fine work, and are waiting for the sun of righteousness and freedom to arise and shine, which, they believe, is sure to crown their labors.

We find there is a section of country here, called Lebanon, that is ruled by a Christian governor. He is appointed once in five years by the sultan ; but the European powers dictate in the matter, and will not allow a Mohammedan to be appointed. This territory includes the range of the Lebanon Mountains, also the Anti-Lebanon, and the valley lying between. These mountains I have referred to in writing up Baalbec, and spoke of the improvement of the people of that place, especially the female portion.

I believe the Christian nations should and will erelong make a demand on Turkey, and not allow the iron hand of superstition to grind the people any longer. Beyrout in appearance is not old enough to be called antique nor young enough to be giddy. Its early history has nothing startling. It was at one time destroyed in consequence of its rebellion against Antiochus VII., but afterwards was rebuilt by the Romans, and named Augustus Felix after the Emperor Augustus, with a view to pleasing his friends.

Herod Agrippa at one time embellished it with baths and theatres, and caused combats of gladiators to be exhibited, etc. After the destruction of Jerusalem, Titus caused numerous Jews to enter the lists against each other. At one time it was held by the Druses. In 1840 it was bombarded by an English fleet without much damage, and recaptured for the Turks. But the days of war are passing by, yet there are more swords than ploughshares in Syria to-day. But we expect to see the transformation take place soon, when the people will rejoice.

X.

According to our itinerary we should have left Beyrout the 15th; but the running of the steamers had lately been changed; and we were obliged to wait until the 19th, giving us some eight days in Beyrout. But the American consul and our college friends made it so pleasant for us that the time passed very quickly.

Our party have avoided as far as possible travelling on the Sabbath. Only once before since we left have we encroached on holy time. When we left Port Saïd, we took steamer for Jaffa Sunday afternoon; and Sunday, the 19th, our steamer was to leave Beyrout for Athens at twelve o'clock. Rev. Mr. Horton of our party preached at nine in the morning to the college boys and others. Text, "I am not ashamed of the gospel of Christ."

At 11.30 we were all on board the "Senegal," a French steamer, four hundred and twenty feet long and 600 horse-power engines. It was the finest running boat we have yet had the privilege of travelling on. She runs through the blue waters of the Mediterranean like a duck, counting off about fifteen knots per hour. She is the personification of neatness, and the cuisine is excellent; and, after having so much Syrian and gum Arabic *table d'hôte*, we certainly enjoyed the French cooking. Many of our Beyrout friends came on board to bid us farewell; and, as we steamed out of the harbor, we could look back upon College Hill, and see the waving of handkerchiefs, which we returned as the last good-by.

We took a south-west course, and before sundown we were running along near the island of Cyprus. This island, one hundred or more miles long, is Turkish territory; but the English government has leased it, paying ninety thousand pounds per year. This was done as a military strategy. The English hold the north end of the Mediterranean with Gibraltar. The south end is held by this island. They keep a part of their navy and soldiers here, and can throw them very quickly into Egypt or anywhere in the Turkish provinces.

Monday morning the sun rose clear, a fresh breeze from the west, and the sea looked like watered silk, while our engines in their quiet way are pushing us through the blue waters. Everybody seems happy. You can have a cup of coffee from 7 to 9, and breakfast at 10, lunch at 1, dinner at 6, and tea and crackers at 8.30. Retire when you please.

About three o'clock in the afternoon we were coasting along the shore of Asia Minor. At our right the hills and mountains had thrust themselves, as it were, down into the sea, forming a promontory. Back in the distance could be seen the snow-capped mountains. The country looked rugged; but no doubt there were many fertile valleys and plains nestled among those rugged cliffs that stood ready to be the first to greet all mariners and passengers going up and down the Mediterranean.

Tuesday we are to pass the island of Rhodes. Finding the morning clear and bright with a smooth sea, about 9 A.M. we bear to the right, and run up into a beautiful bay, with hills and elevations on both sides of us, studded with trees and foliage of green. In some places the channel is quite narrow, reminding us of different places on the Hudson. About one hour's sail, and we anchor at a modern-looking town of Vathy, on the island of Samos. Our steamer put off and takes on merchandise here, and will remain the rest of the day, giving us a chance to go ashore. No backsheesh will be called for here; for, as they say, every one is rich.

Samos is Turkish, but, like Lebanon, has a right to a Christian governor, the European powers dictating in the matter; and we see no mud houses and squalor that is seen in most of the Turkish provinces. It is said that they make the finest wine in the world, that being the main product. Our steamer is loading it by the quantity. They import as it were nothing, but export much. Hence we can understand how they grow wealthy. We take on three hundred and fifty casks that weigh almost a ton to a cask. We have wandered upon the side of the mountain, looked the people over, and talked with those that could talk English. We see no veiled women, the dress of all being quite American; and we are delighted with Vathy. The island of Samos, which is seventy miles in circumference, the people pay the Turkish government two thousand pounds a year for, and then run things as they please. A cannon was fired at sundown, and the sweet notes of the bugle sounded, notifying the people that twilight was soon to settle down upon them. There are forty thousand people on the island.

At 7.30 the "Senegal" weighed anchor, and headed

her prow down the bay; and the crescent-shaped town that had climbed from the shore up the mountain a mile or more threw out its lights, and our farewell look at Vathy was a beautiful one, and will be long remembered.

Wednesday morning before we had left our cabin our steamer had cast anchor; and the jabbering of the native boatmen was all about as we hurried on deck, and found that we were in front of a town of some twenty thousand inhabitants, being the city of Smyrna. We have been sailing over some of the route that Paul went over when going up to Jerusalem. (See Acts xx.) John, in Revelation, speaks of Smyrna as having endured. (See Rev. ii. 8, 9.)

Smyrna stands next to Constantinople in commercial importance, being second in the Turkish empire. It has a fine harbor, buildings stretching along the bay for miles, then gradually rising back on the hills that line the coast. On the top of the hill are the ruins of an old stone castle or fort. South of this you will find the tomb of Polycarp, the first martyred bishop. Smyrna was once a walled city. The old ruined wall and stone aqueduct that formerly supplied the city with water are among the things of interest that you will want to look over. We find Smyrna remarkably neat for this country. Good water and plenty of it, and good sewerage.

The bazaars are far above the average of those we have seen since entering the Turkish territory. Many fine stores with many French goods in them are to be found here. There are two things here that are household words with us in America; that is, Smyrna rugs and figs. We have seen stacks of the former, and have had fine figs at our command. The American Board of Missions have a hold on the people here in Smyrna. Rev. Mr. Bartlett, who at one time preached at Morrisville, Vt., is at the head, with several helpers. The work is among the young. We have visited the mission, and the missionaries have called on us on board the "Senegal."

The sultan of Turkey is strong in his Mohammedan belief; and he is watching the influence that true Christianity is having on his people with a jealous eye, and is bound to hold them with rods of iron.

Thursday morning we take small boats for the shore, and then take the street-cars down the bay for a mile, where we find a special train for Ephesus, some forty-eight miles. We take an easterly course, finding our way through the hills that line the shores of the Mediterranean, and soon begin to open out upon a broad plain. We first go through a place called Paradise; but we enter it through a large burying-ground, which seemed rather suggestive. But on we go; and the valley becomes miles in width, covered with fig-trees, some olive vineyards, etc. Off at your right you will see trains of camels coming and returning to and from Smyrna, loaded with grain and merchandise from and for the interior. Farther on you will see large herds of sheep. From these come the wool for the Smyrna rugs.

After one and one-half hours of enjoyable riding,

the hills and mountains that have guarded us on each side seemed to come together close to us, and form a gateway through which we pass, coming into a valley nearly surrounded by hills, where once was the great city of Ephesus, referred to in Acts xviii. 19. To-day there are only two or three hundred people. See what John says, Rev. ii. 4–10. But you can ride miles and over hundreds of acres, and see old ruins. One thing very peculiar is, as you go into the town, every old column and minaret seems to be topped out with a stork, standing there in its loneliness. The tip of the wings and tail is black, while the rest of the body is white.

The modern name of this place is Ayassacook. I think it ought to be Storkville. The nests of the storks are on these columns. A short distance west of this little village is quite an elevation, on which are the ruins of an old Roman castle. You ascend to that point, and you get a view of the whole valley. Down at the base on the south side are quite respectable ruins of an old mosque. A little farther on you will see men at work excavating, and it proves to be the site of that wonderful temple of Diana of the Ephesians.

They have decided to learn more of that building that Demetrius stirred up such a commotion about among the people, regarding the shrines of Diana, and are spending money in digging over the ruins. I have always admired the town clerk they had at that time, and looked about for some of his documents, but was not able to find them. His counsel, you will remember, was not to be rash. If Paul had done anything wrong, they had the law. He seemed to be level-headed. (See Acts xix. from 35th verse.)

From this elevation, looking west about two miles distant, you see the waters of the Mediterranean. Ephesus used to be a great seaport and commercial city; but Smyrna has stolen its thunder, and all this kind of traffic is at Smyrna to-day. Righteousness exalteth a nation, but sin is a reproach to any people. The best thing we saw at Ephesus was a comfortable little hotel where we went for lunch. The proprietor showed us his register for 1878, where General U. S. Grant had booked his name. He felt quite proud of having had so noted a guest.

3 P.M. found us back at Smyrna. At four we were steaming out of the bay. Friday about noon we reached Thessalonica, a town of a hundred and twenty thousand people, one-half Jews. It is beautiful for situation, forming a crescent around the bay. A portion of the place rises up to quite a height; yet there is much level or rolling land in and beyond the city; and it has an extra fine farming country back of it. The business is largely trade with the surrounding country. It has one cotton mill, and they would like a woollen mill to make flannel. Wool, cotton, and cereals are their main products. Our steamer remained at Thessalonica until Saturday morning. The Congregational party went ashore, and took carriages through the city, found many good buildings, thought it a comparatively neat town. We saw some native Albanians. They wore a white pleated skirt, very full, coming down about to the knees, reminding me of ballet girls.

The dress of the people of the country we have been travelling through the last six weeks has for its watchword "variety." You see everything that fashion is heir to, colors vying with the rainbow ; and you can be entertained at any time by standing on the corner of the street or sitting on your hotel piazza, and watch the surging crowds as they pass by.

Reaching Athens nearly finishes our travels on the Mediterranean, having been on her waters in all some fifteen days. She has behaved beautifully, though we understand she is capable of getting her back up and making things lively; but she has lately been on her good behavior, and passed us over her smooth waters, giving us a charming ride. At times we were out of sight of land, but usually we could see the foot of hills and mountains, sometimes towering so high as to hold the frost of winters firmly in their grasp. We have enjoyed many an hour on deck, watching the light shade to crimson, blue, gray, and green, changing like the kaleidoscope,— the brilliant rays of morning, the soft and beautiful shades of twilight. This and the pleasant chatting with those who but three months ago were strangers to us, but now are cherished friends,— all this environment rushes in upon us to fill the book of memory with a richness that will be a joy to us as time rolls on.

We have been sailing through the archipelago, and have passed the plains of Marathon, where the Athenians fought and won that terrible battle with great odds against them with Darius the Persian. Saturday night we were informed that we should reach the Piræus, which is the port of Athens, at five o'clock Sunday morning. Wishing to get a view of the harbor and city that was at one time the wonder of the world, I decided to be on deck at four o'clock. The boat proved to be an hour late. Therefore, I had a chance to enjoy the whole scene. When I reached deck, the hills on each side were gathering down upon us; but erelong we spied in the distance the Acropolis with its ragged top, standing back from the shore, but showing us the location of Socrates's home. Soon on the shore we could see tall chimneys and a cluster of buildings which proved to be the Piræus. The "Senegal" steamed up the harbor, and anchored not very far from shore. Boatmen were on hand, and men, women, and baggage were soon landed on *terra firma;* and we soon found ourselves in some fine landaus, and were driven five miles over as fine a road as is usually found in any country. The cars run up to the city; but carriages seemed to be the order of the day, landing us at the Grand Hotel, where we found breakfast ready and everything more than satisfactory. Will give you a picture of Athens in my next letter.

LETTER FROM GREECE.

ATHENS, May 29, 1895.

The last port we left before reaching this place was on Turkish territory. The streets were full of Turkish trousers, turbans, and the fez, with all the brilliant colors that Persian dyes would make. But, when we reached the Piræus, a place of three thousand nine hundred people, which is the front door and vestibule of Athens, we found that the baggy Turkish trousers had wonderfully diminished in size. The brilliant colors had become sombre, the turbans and the fez had been laid away in the archives of the past, and the American hat is touched as you meet the people. For a little spice you would occasionally meet an Albanian with his white pleated skirt coming down to within some four inches of the knee, with tight leggings coming up as high as the law will allow. The full Grecian sleeves and waist trimmed with gold lace, the sleeves hanging down below the elbow, made a very jaunty suit, — something that will cause you to leave all the rest of mankind, and gaze till your curiosity is satisfied.

When we landed and met the people of this country, we noticed that the gesticulating, exciting motions we had been accustomed to were missing; but everything they said was Greek to us, and all we could say was nonentenday. However, we prefer the Athenians to the Turks and Syrians.

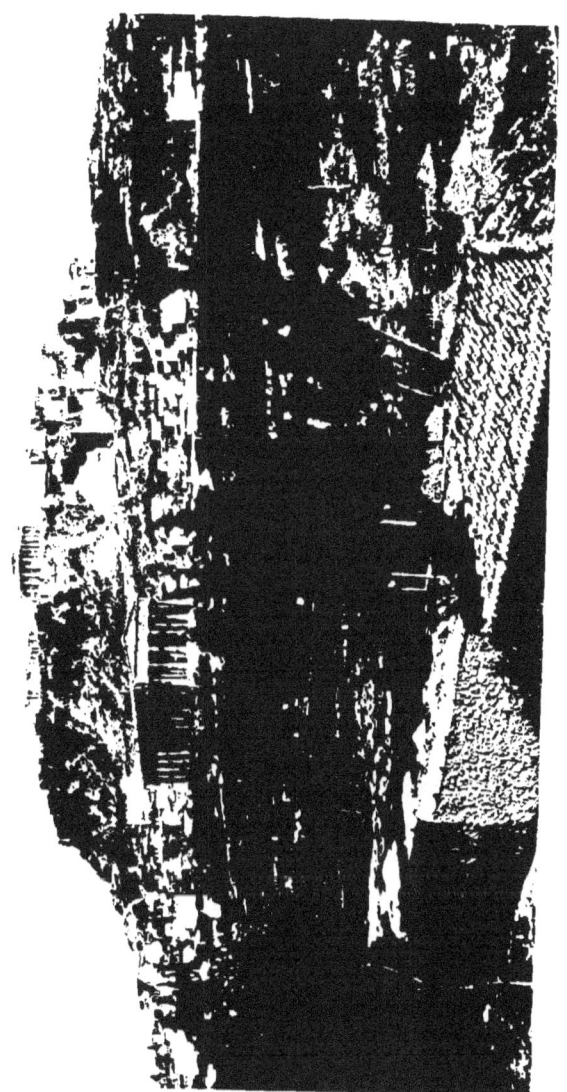

ACROPOLIS AT ATHENS.

The Piræus is modern and full of thrift, has a fine harbor full of merchant vessels, and is doing a large inland business. In ancient times one of the old kings walled in the Piræus with Athens, running the walls from the coast up around Athens, making the two places one, although they are some four or five miles apart. As you take the drive up the valley from the Piræus, you will see the relics of the old walls. When you reach the city, you will find there is an old and new Athens. The historical and beautiful Athens was once the hub of the world. Art, science, literature, poetry, and sculpture were once centred here; and, as you walk about the city, you are constantly being reminded that the glory of these things has not entirely departed. From the ruins of the old temples they are digging up the Corinthian, Doric, and Ionic columns and architecture.

In the new and beautiful buildings this same style is being reproduced. This city reminds us of Rome in many things. Rome has one advantage; and that is an abundance of water, which Athens is not favored with. Statuary abounds in both cities. You will see Plato, Socrates, Demosthenes, and that class of men, sitting or standing in the public places or connected with the public buildings of Athens.

If you are going to look over the city, the first thing to do is to go with me to the Acropolis, the word meaning height of the city. Nature held out a helping hand to the kings, and threw up a conical hill some two hundred feet high, not round, but oblong. The top is of lime-rock or granite and flat, with a surface of some two acres, being precipitous except on the west side. The kings threw a wall around the edge of the top of this elevation, and on the top built the temples. The entrance on the west side was guarded by what is called Enneapzion Pilasgikon, or nine gates. This place became the home of the Athenian kings. Here they sat in judgment, and assembled their councils.

Later these were removed to the town, and the Acropolis devoted to the gods. These temples were at one time destroyed by the Persians, and were rebuilt in greater splendor than ever by Pericles. The Pantheon was its pride, and when at its best, with its white marble and gold, with the Erechtheion, was the glory of the city, and has gone into history as one of the wonders of the world. Its present destruction, with part of its temples standing and the ground strewn with broken columns, is due to an officer of a besieging army firing a bomb into a magazine of powder that was stored on the Acropolis.

As you stand there, looking down the bay, you see the Piræus. Beyond, some thirty miles, you see Acrocorinthus, showing the location of Corinth. As you turn and look south, at the foot of the hill is the theatre of Bacchus. This was without a covering; and the stage was at the bottom of the hill, while the seats were in amphitheatre style, coming up to the upright walls of the Acropolis. The seats were of stone. In the first rows were marble chairs for the great men of the nation. In the centre was a marble platform in which sat the king. The theatre would seat thirty thousand. At the right was a colonnade built, where they could go between the acts and promenade at pleasure. A little farther to the right was the Odeion, a small theatre built of stone in the same way, only it was covered.

We are now looking over old Athens. Much of it has been demolished and covered up, and has become a pasture for the goats. Looking west again a few hundred rods, you will see the hill of the Muses. As you commence to rise, the hill is a perpendicular rock. Into this rock there have been made prison rooms, with three doors to enter. Here was where Socrates was imprisoned, and ended his life by taking hemlock. On the top of this elevation is the tomb of Philopappos. Looking north-west only a short distance from the Acropolis is what was in ancient times and is now called the Areopagus, or Hall of Mars. Paul went on to Mars' Hill. (See Acts xvii.) A few of us went there. The day we arrived being the Sabbath, the Rev. C. P. Mills, of Newburyport, read the last part of that chapter. It seemed like hearing direct from the author.

A little west of Mars' Hill is another elevation, with stone steps leading up to it. Up those steps went Demosthenes, when he spoke to the people of Athens. As you stand on the Acropolis and view the landscape over, you can see in your mind's eye those giants moving among the people, with ideas in advance of their time, which have rung down through the ages.

Turning around more to the north-west, looking down at the base of the Acropolis is where the markets were located, and where it is supposed Paul often went and proclaimed the Christian doctrine to the Athenians. A little beyond is the temple or tomb of Theseus, which is said to be the best preserved relic of old Athens, with its Ionic columns all intact.

We have been gazing mostly at our feet. Let us now take a sweep around the country. At the south some eight miles lies Mount Hymettus. From this section came the famous honey of Hymettus. We have had it on our table every day since we arrived. Around to the east is Mount Pentelikon. From these two mountains come the beautiful marble that formed the temples and buildings of old Athens, and the new city is indebted to those mountains for the beauty that attracts the stranger's eye to-day. These mountains seem to encircle Athens, forming a beautiful background, standing as it were like guardians of her welfare.

Just east of the town is Mount Lykabettos, a small, conical hill, about six hundred feet high, on which is the chapel of St. George. This hill is very symmetrical, with green foliage two-thirds the way up. The other third is of lime-rock and granite, and with the white chapel on top is one of the first things the stranger will notice as he comes into the city. Before leaving the Acropolis, you will see beyond Mars' Hill the hill of the Nymphs, on which is a beautiful observatory, built by the Baron Sina, of Vienna. He also gave the city a beautiful building called the Academy of Science, of which I will speak later.

From our standpoint we have a fine view of the new part of Athens. Away to the east it is beginning to climb up to Mount Lykabettos, and north it is stretching out across the plain with fine streets and avenues and foliage of green, making a pretty picture. Here we find a great many pepper-trees. Their beauty is known to every one that has ever seen them. The streets are nearly all macadamized, and would be a paradise for the cyclist. Let us now return to the Grand Hotel, standing on the Place de la Constitution, where you find all the best hotels of the city, as well as the king's palace. Take a carriage, and go east by the palace, then south ten minutes, and you come to the Stadium. This is where in olden times they used to have their chariot and foot races, the throwing of trays, etc. Nature did her part in forming this institution and art the rest. It is a flat piece of ground of some two acres, with an embankment around it some twenty feet high, in the form of a horseshoe, being narrow at the heel, leaving a place to enter. Most of this was natural, though the heel seemed to have been fashioned by man.

This embankment formerly contained marble seats, and was capable of seating fifty thousand people. In some of Athens's misfortunes and depressions these games were given up, and the marble carried away and used for other purposes. But the city has decided to renew those exhibitions, and are now putting in the marble seats. They believe it will attract tourists and draw a large number of people to the city.

At the end opposite the entrance is an underground passage-way leading to the outside of the embankment as well as outside the city. The victors returned to the city the way they came in, crowned with laurels while the vanquished went out through this tunnel, and never showed their faces in the city again. The Stadium will not be completed until next season. Therefore, we will retrace our steps, and take a drive down the Boulevard de la Université, and return on the Rue du Stade, two streets that run to and from the king's palace, parallel with each other, lined with pepper-trees.

Here you will find some of the finest buildings in Athens. One of the first that will meet your eye is the Academy of Science, built by Baron Sina, of Vienna. This is of Pentelic marble, with Ionic colonnades and in classic Grecian style. As you enter to go up the broad marble steps and walk, you can, if you choose, be introduced to Plato sitting at your left and Socrates at your right. The marble and gold before you will thrill you with admiration. The group in the pediment of the central structure represents the birth of Athena. The gables are filled with statuary. As you enter the main hall, high up on the walls are beautiful paintings by Griepenkerl, of Vienna,— Prometheus lighting his torch in the presence of Athena, Prometheus breathing life into man in the presence of Athena, etc.

At the farther end of the hall stands Baron Sina. He must have been a fine subject to have operated upon; but, aside from that, the workmanship is exquisite, and will hold you spell-bound as you look upon it. It was executed, as was much of the other statuary, by Drosos. Beyond this building is the

University of Athens, standing in its beauty and wonderful capacity, with sixty professors and some two thousand students.

It is organized on the German system, and is said to be doing fine work. It has a library of one hundred thousand volumes. In this section of the city is the museum, which it will be well for you to visit when you have time. It abounds with statuary, and much of it was very fine. Old Neptune attracted my attention as much as anything. He looked as though he had just come up out of Plymouth Pond, with his locks dripping, spear in his hand, and a big fish by his side.

We must hurry on, for it is time for lunch, but must call your attention to the Palace Olion built by Dr. Schliemann and now occupied by his widow, also on our return we might step into the House of Parliament, which is a stately-looking building, though the inside looks a little rusty.

Greece is poor, and has hard work to raise money enough to pay the interest on her debt. Dr. Schliemann, whose residence I have just made mention of, was the great explorer of the plains of Troy; and we expect to see much that he found there in the museum at Constantinople. While at Athens, we took a drive one afternoon to Eleusis, ten miles from Athens, going over what is called the sacred way.

Eleusis is a small town, mostly Albanians living there. It was the home of Æschylus, the earliest of the three great tragedians. When a little way out of the city, we stopped, and looked over the old olive-tree planted by Plato when he first began to teach at thirty years of age. This would make it over fifteen hundred years old. It had an immense hollow trunk, with a few limbs and sprouts growing, but it looked toothless, shrivelled, and shorn of its beauty. It has been grazed and barked by the wheel of time. The olive-tree has a wonderful tenacity for life, and when the funeral obsequies will be held over it is uncertain.

The ruins of the temple of mystery are at Eleusis, aud in its day the temple must have been attractive and of great capacity. No one was ever allowed to enter or join the order that would divulge the tenets of the organization. Of course, the ladies would not care to become members.

If you wish for a charming drive, go to Eleusis. The last part of the drive as you go around the Bay of Eleusis is lovely. You are in plain view of the Bay of Salamis, where Xerxes, with his fifteen hundred war vessels, fought the Grecians, who had six hundred; and the old king had the satisfaction of sitting up on the shoulder of the mountain that comes down to the sea, and see his navy annihilated by the Grecians, although he had great advantage in numbers.

We returned to our hotel, having had a fine drive of twenty miles. No better roads can be found anywhere than about Athens. In the evening Mr. Cummer, of Michigan, one of our party, and myself went out and looked over the electric light station, and found Babcock boilers, Westinghouse engines, and Edison system all doing good work. They have commenced right by putting their wires all underground. Wages in this city for common laborers are $2.50 per month and board. We are pleased with Athens, but down goes my pen for this time.

Hope to be able to take you into Constantinople in a few days.

LETTER FROM CONSTANTINOPLE.

JUNE 5, 1895.

Wednesday, May 29, our steamer was to leave Athens, or the Bay of Piræus, at 7 P.M. for Constantinople, a sail of forty-five hours. It was an Austrian boat, the "Hungaria," medium size, and not first-class. The cabins were for four instead of two, and the boat was packed from stem to stern. Therefore, the ladies and gentlemen were separated. I at once selected my quartette, and had it understood if any one became sonorous in the night he should be reported at once to the captain. We had on board counts and countesses, and people that never heard of a count, all nationalities mixed up together.

When we drove down from Athens and took small boats out to the steamer, the heavy black clouds were hanging on the mountains, and looked as though the breezes would be down upon us before morning.

However, in due time we were all packed away for a comfortable night; but early in the morning we found ourselves in the Ægean Sea, with high running billows, facing a gale. There were two men in our cabin that prided themselves on being good sailors. They walked the deck and dining-room of the "Normannia" every day when crossing the Atlantic; but Thursday, the 30th, it was too windy to be on deck, and the dining-room was anything but satisfactory.

The bunks in the cabin seemed to be the only place of comfort in the boat. The ladies' cabins were on deck, and they had a lively time. Some made their wills, others turned over their letters of credit for safe keeping, etc. However, the "Hungaria" kept on her course; and about 3 P.M. we left the boisterous sea to play havoc with others, and we were in the Dardanelles, where we found smoother waters, and the dining-room became a place of comfort, and the deck was filled with people.

In the evening our engine broke down, and detained us some three hours. It was lucky for us that it did not happen when on the sea.

The next morning we were passing the plains of Troy. Here was where the Greeks besieged the city, but could not take it until they played a shrewd game on the Trojans. They made an immense wooden horse, inside of which were some Greeks, then feigned a retreat. The Trojans came out to gather up what was left, and among other things drew into the city the wooden horse. In the night out came the Greeks, and opened the gates of the city. In came the Grecian army, and the thing was ended.

When we left the Dardanelles, we sailed into the Sea of Marmora, which extends to the Bosphorus. About noon the Marmora had narrowed down, the shore of Asia was on our right, and Europe on our left; and away in the distance at the left could be seen Constantinople, stretching along up the sea, domes and minarets by the hundred. The mosque Suleimon with her six minarets, and the S. Sophia with her dome piercing the sky one hundred and seventy-five feet, one hundred and eight feet at the base, occupying some fifty thousand square feet, are objects that will set the Yankee tongue in motion; and he wishes to know what those wonderful buildings are and where are the people that use them, but you can satisfy him by giving the name and promising to take him in later.

Constantinople lies on rolling land. In some places she goes up from the sea and Bosphorus quite abruptly, giving a bold appearance. In other places she retires in a more modest manner. As an Oriental town, she has more than the usual amount of trees and foliage, which add to her beauty.

On her right as we sail up the bay is Scutari. This is Asiatic Turkey. On the hill away in the distance is located the girls' college and school belonging to the American Board, which is doing a grand work.

Before going ashore, we might as well go up the Bosphorus and Golden Horn and the sweet waters of Europe. The Bosphorus connects the Sea of Marmora with the Black Sea, being eighteen miles in length and from one to three miles wide.

As you come up to the landing, you turn to the right, leaving the Sea of Marmora. Entering this noted channel, take a small steamer, and you will have a beautiful sail up and back, both banks being lined with buildings. Perhaps in forty minutes at your right you will see the girls' college that I have referred to. Dr. Dunning preached to the girls last Sabbath, much to their satisfaction; and it is evident that they will give the doctor a call. Our party were all invited there the 4th to an afternoon spread, resulting in a splendid time, full of enjoyment.

The land on either side of this channel is picturesque of itself, rising somewhat abruptly in places, but fertile to the top, scattered over with Oriental trees and shrubbery. Among these are nestled the houses, as well as many fine and imposing buildings. About as soon as you turn into the Bosphorus at your left from the shore, up back as far as you can see are the sultan's grounds and palaces and beautiful stables for his horses.

Upon this elevation, overlooking the waters of Marmora and the Bosphorus, live the king of Turkey and almost all of his relatives; yet I have seen many a humble American with a happier-looking face than wears this king in all his regal splendor.

A little farther on, and you pass a little mosque that cannot be surpassed for beauty. On this art and skill seemingly have spent their energies. This is where the king goes to worship, although he has a rule which he follows; that is, to worship once a year in every mosque in the city.

Farther up the channel at your left, high up on the hill, standing up boldly, is Robert College, putting in her hard knocks for truth, righteousness, and good will to men; and she is, no doubt, an eyesore to the sultan.

America is at fault in one thing. She ought to put the best man the nation affords here as consul, a man level-headed, that will stand up for righteousness and at the same time go for business. This she has not done. The Turks are wily, polite, and treacherous. Our consul here, they say, loses his head. I do not think he is anywhere up to the man at Beyrout.

The German consul is doing much toward introducing German goods into Turkey, but the people say they prefer American goods when they can get them. I met a lady yesterday that has all her butter from Waterbury, Vt., coming through in tubs in first-class condition.

But I am getting off my track; and, as we are now nearly at the upper end of the Bosphorus, if you will look back down the coast, you will see that Constantinople with its suburbs is a long city, being about thirty miles in length, resting on this channel and the Sea of Marmora, and containing about one million of people. This city is built largely of wood, some of the buildings being six and seven stories high. While there are many fine-looking buildings, yet a majority of them look rusty, never having seen paint or whitewash. The earthquake, some ten months or more ago, shook them up badly; and you can see many of the scars to-day.

When we return to the landing and stand facing the city, we see the course of the Bosphorus to the right and the Golden Horn going to the left, up through the city. This is where the three waters meet, — Marmora, Bosphorus, and Golden Horn.

Stamboul, the old part of Constantinople, lies to the left of the Horn as you ascend its waters, also running down the shore of Marmora. This part of the city was once the capital of the Greek empire.

TURKISH LADIES.

Now, to go up the Golden Horn, we will take a kaik. There are said to be thirty thousand of these little boats in the waters around Constantinople. They are long and narrow, being twenty feet or more in length, and look like an Indian canoe. They carry four people, who are seated in the bottom of the boat, four oars with two men to handle them, and they row for dear life; it is fun to go skipping over the waters of the Golden Horn.

The Horn, where it enters the sea, is about one-half mile wide, and is spanned by a pontoon bridge; but we get into our kaik just above this bridge, and in a short time we go under another bridge, and pass some ten or fifteen old war vessels, which are about all the navy Turkey possesses.

The Horn is six miles long, and the boatmen will hustle you over its waters in about fifty minutes. It grows narrow as you ascend, the last two miles being the sweet waters of Europe, and is a place of great beauty, — groves, villas, places of amusement, etc., all along its banks, — and goes meandering its way to the end.

Friday is a gala-day. The Turkish ladies are out, and these waters are literally covered with boats.

It is a great place for picnics. We saw one place where they were having a jolly time roasting the whole carcass of a sheep; they had a stick run through it lengthwise, and were turning it over a big fire of coal, as you would turn a grindstone. I could see by their expression that they had an eye for a good dinner.

Mutton is king in this country, and I will just

call your attention to the meat wagons that run through Constantinople; and, if you wish to go into the business here, it will cost you but a trifle to rig up a cart. Take two boards about three feet square, and hang them on a horse, one each side, have some hooks put in on which to hang your roasts, steaks, liver, chops, etc., and you are all right for business. Then you will see many cheaper arrangements than that. A man takes on his shoulder a pole some ten feet long. On this he hangs calves' heads, pluck, lights, and liver, — some things you might relish, but much that you would not. This fellow travels about, furnishing any one that sees fit to buy.

A man gets full of these quaint things in travelling through these Oriental towns.

I informed you not long ago that we had reached the climax on dogs at Damascus, but I should have waited until we reached this place. The first day we arrived we took carriages, and rode through the streets of Constantinople one and a half hours. We counted seven hundred and fifty dogs, and it was not much of a day for dogs, either. The dogs have their own territory; and, if a dog gets off that on to another dog's ground, they give him Hail Columbia until he gets back again. Fifteen in one pile is the largest cluster I have seen yet, but am prepared for anything in the way of canines, and also intend to keep in that frame of mind until I leave the Turkish empire.

The great Turkish annual festival "Bairam," lasting some days, commenced Monday, the 3d. Every well-to-do Mohammedan is expected to buy a sheep at that time, take it home and kill it, and then divide up the meat among the poor, so that every man shall have meat in his house once a year. This is the most Christian thing, in my opinion, the Turks are guilty of doing. The 2d of June we noticed the sheep were coming into the city from all directions by the hundreds and thousands, and were soon informed what was coming.

The sultan commences the slaughter by drawing the knife gently across a sheep's neck ; and, as he was to be at a certain mosque or castle at six o'clock that morning, we decided to take a ride before breakfast, and were on the ground early, getting a good position. They had out the military. The sultan rode in a carriage drawn by four horses, and gold lace seemed to be abundant. The officers and horses in the Turkish army appear to be covered with tinsel, while the soldiers were plain in dress and appearance.

The sultan is fifty-six years old, and beginning to show iron-gray in hair and whiskers. His boys rode in carriages behind the king, each one having a carriage by himself. One of them, the youngest, attracted our attention as being a fine little fellow.

When we arrived here, and were fairly settled in our hotel, we were called on by Dr. Herrick, a brother of Dr. L. H. Cobb's wife, who has been a missionary here and at Massavan in the interior many years. We accepted an invitation from him to go and spend Saturday night at his house, which we enjoyed exceedingly, learning much of the work of the missionaries, also of the people.

Two of his native teachers at Massavan were arrested some eighteen months ago, accused of plotting against the government, and were sentenced to be hung; but the doctor succeeded in getting another hearing, and cleared them by fleeing the country.

Jealousy and ignorance have no limit among the Turks. A man telegraphed to Germany for a pulley to run so many revolutions, and he was arrested at once because the word "revolution" was in the telegram.

All letters going out of the country, if directed to editors, are examined, and destroyed if not satisfactory. So we have sent all letters, if possible, through the British post-office. Not a scrap of anything can be printed, not even an auction notice, without first going before the censor.

We have visited the Seven Towers that stands at the south-west part of the city, close by the Sea of Marmora. This is a large enclosure with a high wall and towers on the corners, some two hundred feet high. This place at one time was occupied by the janizaries, and many a king lost his head here. There is a small open court inside, called the place of heads. Seven thousand were beheaded at one time, and the heads piled in here. The blood ran in trenches out of the castle. On one side are prison rooms or dungeons. At one time Lord Byron occupied one of them. Near these rooms is what is called the well of blood, where they threw their slaughtered victims. This well is connected by a channel with the Sea of Marmora, so everything went out into sea.

We came to this point on a railroad tram skirting along the seashore, and saw much of the old walls of the city Stamboul. Gala and Pera form the main part of the present Constantinople. In Galata, upon high ground, stands the Galata Tower, one hundred and fifty feet high, and is a grand place to get a view of the city. In the Middle Ages it was called the Tower of Christ or of the Cross. It is now used as a fire-signal station, using flags in the day-time, lanterns by night. The alarm of fire is given by firing a cannon seven times, and then signal the location from the tower.

The dress of the people has changed here within a few years. While one-half or more are Mohammedans, yet you see but little Turkish dress excepting the fez. The rest of the dress is largely American.

They have here what they call esnap. We should call them labor organizations. Each craft has an order of its own, though in so large a city there will be many branches of the same craft. It is said there are two hundred and fifteen registered orders.

They have their patron god-father, and celebrate once a year to his honor. For instance, Adam is patron to the bakers, Eve to the bath women, Abel to the shepherds, Cain to the grave-diggers, Noah to the ship-builders, etc.

We visited the tombs of the kings, where were buried two sultans and several of their wives. One of the sultans killed himself with the shears, or else the attendants did the work for him. There remains to this day an uncertainty in the matter.

The kings' tombs are covered with wrought

Persian silk, ornamented with gold lace and mother of pearl, and will dazzle your eyes to look at them. The wives' tombs are covered, but not with such splendor. The building was handsome from the word go; and the dome, though small, was exquisitely beautiful.

The mosque S. Sophia, located in Stamboul, is the pride of the Mohammedans of Constantinople. I have already given you an idea of its size; and, as you go inside, you will be impressed with its architectural beauty. It is the third church that has stood on this ground, two having been destroyed. The first was built by Constantine the Great, and was dedicated to Divine Wisdom. The second was built and dedicated to Theodosius. The present one was built by Justinian, costing over one million sterling, and became the centre of the great transactions of state, the emperor's nuptials being solemnized there, and many great and important events.

There are some eight different varieties of marble used in its construction. Troas, Athens, Ephesus, and many other places contributed to the rearing of this edifice. It was turned into a mosque when the Turks conquered Constantinople.

Monday, the 3d, we were all invited to the Bible House to lunch and met many of the missionaries and teachers from the colleges, and had a charming time. Dr. Herrick did the honors at the table in giving us a welcome, and calling out the speakers after the viands were served. Handsome is that handsome does. Taking that as a basis, Constanti-

MOSQUE OF THE SULTAN.

nople will have to look long and wide to find as handsome a man as the doctor. Dr. Dunning was happy in his remarks, as well as several other ministers of our party. Dr. Riggs, sixty-three years on the field, and still at the good work, was with us, occupying the head of the table. We also had the pleasure of meeting Mrs. Bliss, one of the veterans.

Never was there a time when the hearts and hands of the missionaries in Turkey should be stayed up by the American people more than to-day. The cloud of uncertainty is hanging over them. Satan never yields an inch of ground without a struggle. The Turks are drawing the lines closer every year, and the cloud is liable to burst at any time.

The sultan keeps an army in Constantinople of one hundred and fifty thousand.

It being the week of the great Bairam festival, the steamer was not to go up the Danube until Saturday; and, instead of waiting so long, we decided to take a train Wednesday night, and go by rail to Vienna. So we bid good-by to Constantinople June 5 at 7 P.M.

FROM CONSTANTINOPLE TO PARIS.

JUNE 5, 1895.

We bade good-by to Constantinople at 5 P.M. Wednesday. Thursday morn at six we were called upon in our berth for our passports, as we had finished up the territory of Turkey and were ready to enter Bulgaria. We soon satisfied the Bulgarians that we were all right.

From appearances we had a mutual admiration for each other, as we had seen Turks enough; and the Bulgarians, no doubt, had more love for an American than a Turk, as it is only a few years since they freed themselves from Turkish rule by hard-fought battles.

Our engine was soon speeding its way up a beautiful valley, coursing along a beautiful river, nearly as large as the Connecticut. We seemed to breathe a freer atmosphere than in the land we had just left. The towns we passed through looked thrifty, the people happy.

Bulgaria was filled with Greek Christians, and the Turks oppressed them so heavily that they rebelled; and the Russians came in, and helped them gain their freedom.

We could see away ahead in the distance the Balkan Mountains. Over these mountains came the Russians, who with the Bulgarians fought the Turks the whole length of this beautiful valley we are travelling over, driving them clear to Constantinople.

As we passed along, we saw a great many mounds, some twenty-five feet diameter at the base, ten or more feet high, and learned on inquiry they were places where the soldiers were buried. Hence all the forenoon we were passing over a battlefield.

About noon we were in plain view of the mountains over which our big engine was to take us. These mountains seemed to be heavily wooded. The river was beginning to run rapidly; and we found the people were using the water power to run saw-mills, cutting out lumber by the train-load.

Our engine tugged and puffed away vigorously, and at times we moved slowly; but on we went, and about three o'clock were on top of the mountain, where we accelerated our speed, and went plunging down the other side, and at six o'clock we had crossed Bulgaria, and were ready to enter Servia, and of course had to pull out our passports again. Here we had our dinner; and everything was looked over by a set of red-tape fellows, that appeared to have a great weight of responsibility upon themselves. But we took things easily, and soon after our train started we were tucked away in our berth for a good night's rest and sleep, waking early the next morning as we were going into a lovely city, embowered in trees and shrubbery and flowers, located where she could dip her feet into the beautiful Danube; and it proved to be the city of Belgrade, the largest city in Servia. Here is located the king's palace.

In passing through Bulgaria, we became much interested in the people. They seemed industrious, mostly in agricultural pursuits, raising corn and large quantities of winter rye.

Bulgaria is in about the same latitude as Vermont, though I think the crops are more forward than they are in Vermont. The corn was being hoed, and the rye will be ready to harvest in about two weeks.

Here the ladies — for they looked like ladies — worked in the field. They had on their red skirts and Zouave jackets, some of them gayly trimmed, and looked jaunty. We saw but few men in the field. They seemed to do the ploughing, the hoeing being done by the women.

It is a question whether women's rights do not prevail here, and the men are at home making the bread and taking care of the children; but the women and girls looked fresh and healthy, and swung the hoe vigorously.

At every station you see armed police. They wear white coats and caps, blue trousers with gilt buttons and trimmings; and we called them handsome.

We enjoyed our ride through Bulgaria exceedingly. At Belgrade we had to be overhauled again by the government dignitaries, as we were to cross the Danube and enter Hungary and Austria. Hand-bags and everything had to go to the custom-house. Cigars, whiskey, and dynamite seemed to be the articles they were looking for, one about as destructive as the other. The Congregational party had no trouble with anything but the former, and not heavily loaded with that; but, after one hour of unrolling of red tape and haggling away, our train was crossing the Danube over a beautiful, substantial bridge. Passing through Servia in the night, we shall not be able to trumpet forth her glory, but will merely say it is a good country to sleep in, and Belgrade, her capital, looked fine.

After we crossed the Danube, we swept out into a level plain, and soon were lost in a fertile prairie, beautiful land so far as the eye could reach, looking like the West, only it was dotted over with trees that added to its beauty.

In this country the women take the same part in the field as in Bulgaria; and we see but little improvement in farming tools, although we saw them ploughing with ploughs that had mould boards turning the furrow, and two small wheels running in front. On these ploughs there were two and three yoke of oxen, even in light ploughing.

The oxen are the same breed that we saw at Rome,—white, with very large horns running up into the air.

About noon we were running through a country of clay soil and much standing water, and evidently the people had studied gooseology; for no Vermonter ever saw such flocks of geese. One hundred in a flock was no surprise, and we were leaving one flock and running into another for hours.

At one o'clock our train pulled into a spacious depot, and we found ourselves in an American-looking city of five hundred thousand people, called Budapest, lying on the Danube, occupying both sides of the river. We took carriages for the hotel, where we remained one day.

I hardly know how to hold up the town before you that you may get a glimpse of its beauty. The place is but little known, but is rapidly coming to the front, and, if not already, will soon be the finest city in Europe. We come into it sweeping over the Peakos valley. As you look upon the city and beyond, you see the advance guard or picket line of the mighty Alps coming gracefully down to the Danube. On one of these shoulders or arms of the mountain the king has his palace, with his terraced gardens in front, of walks, trees, shrubbery, and flowers, coming down to the Danube, and in the sunlight cast their reflections in its waters, and become the crowning point of a beautiful picture.

The Danube goes sweeping down through the city. One side is level, where the great marts of business have gathered, throwing up massive buildings, not as high as those of Chicago, but from five to eight stories, beautiful in structure, with statuary and ornamentation that the most artistic eye cannot criticise.

Her streets are broad, and look as if they had been swept and garnished. All over her borders are commons and small parks, beautiful with art as well as nature. On the other side of the river, as I said before, are those graceful elevations coming down from the Alps. Upon these has climbed the residence part of Budapest, or at least from appearance the wealthy have gone up there, building fine residences, giving a fine background to the lovely city.

Budapest has considerable manufacturing. It is said to have a model flouring mill, from which the mills of Minneapolis were patterned. She has the finest suspension bridge in the world, spanning the Danube, costing two and a quarter millions. Near the bridge in the square are mounted two splendid statues of distinguished Hungarians. One is Count Stephen Szechenyi, who stands there resting his eye upon two of his great creations: one is the suspension bridge, and the other is the Hungarian Academy of Science. The other statue is Francis Deak, the sage of the country, sitting on a magnificent pedestal. This great statesman succeeded in composing the contentions that had lasted years between Hungary and Austria, and turning them into relations of firm friendship, and has proved a great blessing to both nations.

From the suspension bridge, along the river bank for a long distance, is what is called the Corso. Here runs a beautiful street that carriages are not allowed on in the evening. This is lined with gardens and small parks; and, being on the banks of the river, it is charming. Here you must take a stroll in the evening, and see the brave men and fair women, as well as children, of Budapest. Nowhere in our travels have we seen a people apparently so happy. In going through this Corso, you will see thousands of ladies and gentlemen, also children, in gay attire, some walking, others sitting at their little tables, partaking of some light viands with water or lemonade, chatting merrily. We saw but very little beer or wine, nothing in the way of drunkenness or rowdyism. The people seem to spend much time out doors; and we have seen very few sickly, puny-looking people. God's fresh air and exercise seem to be a panacea for all ills.

Budapest, we understand, has fine schools, museums, art galleries, etc., which we did not have time to visit.

Saturday, June 9, we took our train for Vienna, a run of five hours. Our travel through Austria has been a succession of surprises, finding it a beautiful farming country and scenery unsurpassed anywhere. In travelling through this country, some of our party have had their faces badly twisted by trying to pronounce the names of the stations and towns as we come along, such as Tzaribrab, Szabadka, Kiskoros, etc.; but it probably will not be lasting, and our friends will have no trouble in picking us out when we return.

We reached Vienna Saturday evening, and are quartered at the Hotel Oesterreichischen, and shall remain here until Wednesday morning, when we leave for Paris, being eight hundred and fifty miles. The run is made in twenty-four hours.

Vienna has some sixteen hundred thousand people, and is near the Danube. There are two small tributaries of the Danube that run through the city.

Vienna is known the world over, and it will be foolish for me to weary you in taking you through the city or pointing out things that you are familiar with. You will remember her bread at the World's Fair at Philadelphia in 1876, and we find she still retains the art. So we are enjoying that part of the *table d'hôte*. Vienna at one time was a walled city, that was when her borders were narrow to what they are now; but the city grew, and they built outside, and the wall became of little use and was taken away, and the ground was made into a boulevard, and is called the Ringstrasse. It is a circular street now in the centre of the city, and to go around it will make a trip of some three miles. It is one hundred and eighty-five feet wide. There are three drive-ways for carriages; but each side of the centre one are walks for the people, some forty feet wide, lined each side with trees. These with generous sidewalks next to the buildings make a great thoroughfare, and nearly all of the public buildings and fine residences are on this boulevard. You will find crowds moving on the Ringstrasse at all times of day and night.

One thing new we saw at Budapest, also here in Vienna, is the way they drive many of their single teams. The small wagons, instead of having shafts or thills, as we do in America, have a pole; and the horse is hitched in on the left-hand side as you sit in the wagon. The first one I saw a lady was driving. I came very near going to her and offering her my sympathies. I thought she had been unfortunate, and one of her horses had broken his neck or something else, and she was getting home with one horse the best she could; but she was too lively for me. I was not able to reach her, and was saved the embarrassment; and I soon learned that that was the way they were all driving, but I have no desire to take the fashion home to America.

Sunday, the 9th, we went to the St. Stephen Church. It is the largest cathedral in Austria, tower and spire four hundred and fifty feet high. We heard beautiful music : organ, trumpets, cymbals, and fine voices would take you almost from your feet. We saw them swing the golden censer, burning incense. The rest of it was all Dutch to me.

In one of the chancels of the church was a sarcophagus of Frederic III.

We also took a drive to the king's summer palace on the outskirts of the city, and went through all its gaudy and elegant rooms, one room only twenty-five feet square costing five hundred thousand dollars, finished in mosaic. The grounds and gardens, which were immense in size, were more enjoyable than the house. Here the king entertains his royal guests that come from other countries.

We also visited the Rathhaus, what we would call a town house. It was a building of great capacity, elegant in finish. In it is one hall three hundred feet long, sixty feet wide, with a colonnade and balcony fifteen feet wide, running the whole length, two rows of chandeliers the length of the hall. This is where they have their banquets and public gatherings. In this building the business of the nation is transacted. The building was dedicated in 1883, the two hundredth anniversary of the nation's freedom from the Turks. It cost six millions, and is an attractive ornament to Vienna.

I will call your attention to the Capuchin church. Under this church are large vaults, subterranean passages. Here you will find the royal families of Spain and Austria sleeping their last sleep. There are one hundred and ten already placed there.

Many of the sealed caskets are kept covered with flowers. Maximilian's casket was pointed out to us.

It used to be the custom in olden times, when a lady of the royal family was to be married, to place her here the night before the nuptials. One lady died the next morning from the shock this ordeal gave her.

A few minutes' walk from here we will step into the Augustinian church, and see the beautiful marble statues standing at the tomb of Archduchess Maria Christina, expressing sorrow and benevolence. This was Canova's masterpiece.

As you go around the Ringstrasse, you will notice a large square or park, with fountains, trees, and flowers. Each side there are imposing-looking buildings. One is the museum, the other is the building of natural history. Though you are going to Paris and London and will have a chance to see great things in this line, yet it will pay you to drop in for a half-day at each place.

The mineral collection in the natural history building is said to be the finest in the world. We saw an opal valued at one million. They have collections from all over the world. Saw Vermont granite and marble, Michigan copper, etc.

The parks and gardens of Vienna are delightful. You must be sure and go to the Prater. This is a vast territory just outside the city, shaded with trees and shrubbery, and is fitted up for all kinds of amusement, restaurants and gardens where you can go and get coffee, lemonade, beer, and anything to eat you desire, bands of music playing in all directions. In the evenings thousands upon thousands of people are gathered here for an hour of enjoyment; and, if you wish to see Vienna in all its life and gayety, then go to the Prater.

As you pass through the streets of Vienna, you will be interested in the express wagons. They are drawn by large dogs, usually men or boys with them, but occasionally women are seen doing the trucking of the city. Wednesday, the 12th, at 9 A.M., our train, the Oriental express for Paris, left the station with all hands on board, and went sweeping out into the country of hills and vales, embowered with trees and shrubbery, among which nestled cottages and villas; and occasionally upon some hill-top would be seen a castle, standing like some monarch, owning all he could survey. Farther on comes the broad field, with the tiller of the soil holding possession.

About 2 P.M. we crossed the line into Germany, where we could see the forest that had been planted in rows, beautiful spruces, tall, straight as arrows, fields of clover and grain,— these views constantly changing.

At four o'clock for miles we went sweeping around the outskirts of Munich, covering acres of plain and level country, dotted over with tall chimneys, and from appearance was a real manufacturing city. Iron, cotton, and leather goods are made here, but the greatest of all productions is her beer. Munich beer is known everywhere, and goes out of Munich every day by the train-loads.

Leaving this place, we soon plunged in among the mountains, following down a meandering river for miles.

We had all day long been drinking in the beautiful scenery, and were thankful that scenery was not intoxicating. If it had been, twilight would have found us in bad condition. We looked about for a Joshua to stay the sun, that we might have daylight all the way to Paris; but not a Joshua to be found. So Night spread her mantle over the scene; and we went to our berths, rising at four the next morning, finding the country as beautiful as ever, though the farming lands from appearance not as fertile as Austria and Germany.

We are now in France, and begin to enter the suburbs of Paris. It is evident that Germany and France pay great attention to forestry. The canals, roads, and everything else seem to be lined with trees, besides acres of forests that have been sown or planted.

We shall remain here some six days, and then push on to London.

Our itinerary is about ended for this side of the Atlantic, and I drop my pen here.

Now I have taken you across the Atlantic, through the Mediterranean, Ægean, and Marmora Seas, have been with you on the Nile, traveled over land with you through Italy, Egypt, Palestine, Syria, Greece, Turkey, Bulgaria, Servia, Hungary, Austria, Germany, and into France, and you ought to be able now to travel alone; for I must hurry away to old Vermont, and to a people that I expect have never looked as handsome to me as they will when I next meet them.

If you get into trouble, write me; and I will send

you my passport, and perhaps my letter of credit, although it will probably look thin when I reach Springfield, but there will probably be enough left to help you out. I shall be glad to see you when you return, and we will talk over the sights, scenes, and wonders of the last four months.

PARIS TO SCOTLAND.

When I bade you good-by at Paris June 12, the Oriental party had their faces turned toward New England, and the Vermonters had dreams of the Green Mountain State. Our itinerary was taking us through to New York without any stay of proceedings anywhere. Though our tickets would hold good through the season, the party decided to break up in the beautiful city of Paris, and each one take the reins in his own hands.

Our managers went to their homes, and we were left as free as the breezes of the mountains. For one, I was anxious to see old Scotland, and look over the places where our grandfathers and grandmothers are sleeping, and shake hands with our cousins, see the country where the pure Scotch blood flows freely in the veins of the people,— an article that is current not only in New England, but the world over.

I shall be only too happy to take you to Edinburgh, Glasgow, and through the Trossachs, getting the most we can out of Scotland in the time allowed us. If I do this, I might as well pick up the thread where I dropped it June 12. I shall not detain you very long either in Paris or London.

In Paris the first proper thing to do is to take a small boat up the Seine, stopping at the Eiffel Tower, where you can ascend up into the heavens either in a balloon or go up in the elevator of the tower. The balloon has been started recently as an opposition scheme. It has one advantage in this way, you can go as high as you please. It is held by a rope; and, when you get all of the ethereal regions you care for, they pull it down. However, when you are up in these institutions, Paris is spread out before you like a map; and, if you have taken a guide with you, which is the best thing to do, he will point out all the wonderful things of the city, and, when you return to your hotel, you start out more intelligently than you could without this panoramic view.

As you come up from the boat near the obelisk I referred to in my Egyptian letter, on the Rue Champs Elysées, the finest street or avenue probably in Paris, looking in one direction you see the Tuileries, the other way the Royal Arch of Napoleon.

This arch is a wonderful structure, standing on a slight elevation. The great warrior had the streets laid out so that they radiated from this point like the spokes of a wheel, in order that he might plant his cannon at this arch, and sweep the city in all directions. But the requiem has been chanted over this great general; and he is now sleeping in Hôtel des Invalides, a place you will want to visit before leaving the city. The sun, as it shines through the pale blue and yellow glass, gives a peculiar icy appearance, and will prove to be a picture unlike anything you ever saw before. Here you will see some of the cannon he captured, as well as the flags of other nations that he gathered in his hard-fought battles. On the pavements around his tomb are inscribed the names of the battles he won.

Leading from the altar above to the crypt beneath are flights of steps, at the foot of which is a bronze door with two caryatides in bronze, by Durot, one bearing a sceptre and crown, and the other a globe. Over this door are words taken from Napoleon's will, which your guide will interpret in English, as follows: "I desire that my ashes shall repose on the banks of the Seine, among the French people I have loved so much."

When we consider the thousands that lost their lives to gratify his pleasure and ambition, it sounds rather ironical. Hôtel de Ville is another place that will fill your eyes with admiration. The old building that stood there was commenced in 1533, and was nearly a century in building. It was destroyed in 1871. The Communists had taken possession of it, using it for several months as their headquarters, and had stored in the building large quantities of explosive material. When they were attacked by the soldiers, who shot every one that came out, some foolhardy fellow inside touched off the explosives, which destroyed the building and all there was in it.

In this condition it remained many years, but was finally rebuilt in greater splendor than the original.

The Champs Elysées is very broad, and up the avenue, past the Royal Arch, the people drive to the two-thousand-acre park; and afternoons it is full of people going and coming to that resort. Much of the way of this great avenue it is virtually a park. On either side and in the groves are built theatres and anything and everything for amusement, lighted in the evening with thousands of globe lights. A stroll up and back the Champs Elysées from 8 till 11 P.M. will feed the curiosity of any Yankee that may happen to be in Paris. One evening will be enjoyed at the opera, where you will see the finest opera building in the world.

Place de la Concorde is one of the finest squares in Europe, and carries with it much of historical interest. It was once called Place de la Révolution. Here the guillotine was erected. Louis XVI. lost his head here, also his queen, Marie Antoinette, Madame Roland, Charlotte Corday, as well as hundreds of the nobility.

Some morning early, say eight o'clock,— for that is early in Paris,— you had better visit Les Halles, the great market, situated at the rear of the Rue St. Honoré. This is a wonderful sight, and gives you some idea of the gastronomical powers of the French people, or, in other words, the amount it takes to feed a large city. Le Panthéon, or Sainte Geneviève, is situated on the hill Sainte Geneviève. This church was founded in 1764 by Louis XIV., in accordance with a vow made by him when ill at Metz.

It is built in the form of a Greek cross, and somewhat resembles the Pantheon at Rome. In the vaults of this church have been placed the bones of such men as Voltaire, Victor Hugo, and others of renown. Visiting these old churches in Paris can be carried to any extent one may wish; but most people get full of these things about the second day, and prefer some other diet.

You can step into a meat market where they handle nothing but horseflesh, and see the nice, fat quarters hanging there; also the place where they make sausages out of mule meat.

We can visit the place where they erect the scaffold where they behead the criminals. This is done on one of the main streets of Paris, free to all. Paris has fine streets, which are kept beautifully clean. No city, in my opinion, is ahead of them in that respect.

The people of France are groaning under taxation. Their debt is some four thousand million dollars. They have half a million standing army, another half million that drill a part of the time, also a million men enrolled that they can call out on short notice. The priests draw their money out of the state treasury. Sugar retails at twelve cents per pound, and every pound that is made has to pay a duty to the government. The idea of making beet sugar was first conceived in France. It is said that necessity is the mother of invention.

At the time of the great naval battle of Trafalgar, although Nelson lost his life, the English were victorious on the seas, crushing out the navy of France. They had been having their sugar from the islands. This supply was then cut off; and the people of France became desperate, and were even on the verge of riots. Napoleon called together his greatest chemists, and told them they must devise some way to manufacture sugar; and it resulted in extracting the sweet from the beet.

While in Paris, we visited the Sèvres china works.

Their wares are noted the world over. In their ware-rooms you will see large, elegant pictures painted on porcelain and then fired or burned, which is a very difficult thing to accomplish.

We have feasted our eyes as we have traveled through the Old World on the works of the old masters, and seemingly nothing has outdone the wonderful work of art accomplished by this company. The process of manufacturing their wares was shown to us, and was exceedingly interesting.

Before we leave for London, we will take a day and visit Versailles. This can be done by railroad train or tramway; but the most enjoyable way, if there is a company of you, is to charter a tallyho. It is a ten-mile drive through charming scenery; and, with the jokes, puns, and conundrums that accompany such a drive, it is a thing of anticipation and delight.

Versailles is a place of some fifty thousand inhabitants. The main thing to visit is the palace and grounds, with immense fountains that play only the first Sunday in each month, except on special occasions. Louis XIII. built the first part of the palace, and Louis XIV. added to the original, and employed Le Brun to decorate the entire structure inside and Lenôtre to design and lay out the grounds, expending some forty million pounds.

This palace was used as the seat of the monarchy until 1789, when the Assembly Nationale overthrew the government, giving a free hand to the Revolutionists, who sacked the palace and ended its days as a royal abode. Later Louis Philippe spent six hundred thousand pounds in putting it in repair. He redecorated and converted it into a picture gallery and museum; and, as a whole, it is to-day one of the finest attractions of Paris. While there, you will want to visit the building where the royal carriages are kept, those that have become *passé*. There you will see the most expensive carriage ever built by any king or monarch, which it takes some eight horses to draw. It never was used but three times. Versailles is the first place to visit outside of Paris.

Fontainebleau, thirty-four miles south-west from the city, comes next. There you will find another palace and a wonderful forest of over forty thousand acres. The cheapest and best way to get an idea of the city of Paris or London is to hire a guide, and then take to the tops of the tramways and buses, fare two pennies. By making a few changes, you can go in all directions, and your guide, if a good one, will be continually calling your attention to things of interest; and it also gives you an idea of the broad acres these cities have flung their arms around and appropriated to their use.

Having spent several days here in Paris, we might as well pack our grips, and go through to London. This is about ten hours' ride. You can go by the way of Dover, where it takes but little over an hour to cross the English Channel, which is a terror to all seasick people, or you can go by the way of Newhaven, and be on the channel some three hours. But, in looking over our tickets, I find we are to go by the way of Newhaven. You can leave at 9 A.M. or 9 P.M., the latter taking you through in the night, getting breakfast the next morning in London. The former way you take in the whole thing by daylight, excepting on the channel. There, if you are a good sailor, you are all right. Otherwise you are more likely to let out than take in. However, it makes but little difference. After the ten hours you will find yourself in the largest city in the world ; and you will find no place more convenient and central than Hôtel Metropole, near Trafalgar Square, where stands the statue of Nelson on a very high pedestal.

Around this square are clustered some of the best hotels in London. The Metropole accommodates seven hundred people, and is always full. Here every man must have a silk hat ; and the ladies in the evening are walking fashion plates, with a sprinkling of diamonds thrown in.

It will interest you to watch the head porter, a large, fine-looking fellow, dressed in uniform, from 8.30 to 9.30, as he sends the gentlemen and ladies away from the hotel, mostly to the theatres. The hansoms and four-wheelers, as they call them, fill the square. The porter has a whistle,— one whistle for hansom, two for a four-wheeler. The drivers respond instantly to the call. You tell the porter what you want, and you will be packed into your carriage and sent on your way to your destination before you have time to think about it. He told me he had frequently shipped three hundred in an hour.

I think the best thing to do is to take our trip

into Scotland, and on our return finish up London the last thing before sailing for New York. The train we want leaves Euston Station at 10 A.M., due in Edinburgh at 6.30, a run of four hundred and forty miles in eight and one-half hours. It makes four stops, besides stopping twenty minutes for lunch at Preston. So any school-boy can figure out about how fast we have got to run. When the steam is on, the word "hustle" does not express it. We just went flying, and had to average about one mile a minute; and some of the way they claim to run seventy miles an hour.

We soon left London at our backs, passing through Bletchley, Rugby, Stafford, Crewe, Preston, etc., going through the north of England. This is an old country and under thorough cultivation, with its old English oaks, beeches, etc., and much fine scenery.

After two hours' run, we find we are passing over and among the great coal fields; and we begin to see at our right and left the tall chimneys rolling out their dense volumes of smoke, and we soon learn that the great marts of manufacturing have located in this region. Off at our right is Manchester with her great cotton mills. Beyond are Huddersfield and Leeds, turning out the fine woollens. In another direction is Birmingham, with her great iron-works. Farther on we see at our left a beautiful valley; and we learn on inquiry that it is Windermere, or what is called the English Lakes, and is a fine resort of much gayety and a great place for coaching.

At 4.30 we found ourselves at Carlisle. When we leave there, we enter Scotland, and the picture changes. We find ourselves in a farming country, and everything looks charming: the small white cottages, neat and tidy, and from appearance love reigns within; even the dogs in the front yard smile when we go by, the chickens flap their wings for joy; the cattle in the field are sleek and lazy, either clipping the green grass or chewing their cuds with composure; the horses are willing and strong, as they put their shoulders into the collars, and draw in the large loads of grain and new-mown hay.

You will be delighted with the laddies and lassies of Scotland. The latter can grace the parlor or perform the duties of the kitchen, and, if necessity demands, can help their brothers in the field. It will do you good to look at them. The rose and peach have left their impress on their cheeks. The lass is one of those artless, light-hearted girls that think it is no harm to be kissed when coming through the rye; and, if I were one of the laddies, I should miss no opportunity in walking through the rye with her.

The laddie soldiers are very attractive, with their caps with drooping plumage, white waists and leggings and the Highland plaid skirt, and a sash of the same material coming around under the left arm and up on to the right shoulder, where it is fastened, then hanging down about to the knee. This, with ruddy, fresh, healthy countenance, makes a fine picture; and, if I were an artist, and wished to copy manhood in its fulness, I would certainly go to Scotland.

But you see I have been loitering by the way, and

have said many things that might have been deferred until we reached Edinburgh, where we arrived about on time, and took carriages for the Royal Hotel on Prince Street, which is one of the main streets of the city and the hotel one of the best.

Here we found Carnegie, who is the great iron king of America, and wife. He has done much for Edinburgh. We saw one public building into which he had put two hundred and fifty thousand dollars.

Some think Edinburgh the finest city in Europe. While I do not care to risk my judgment or reputation in the matter, yet I am willing to say that we were delighted with the place and its suburbs.

Lord Lytton has said that it is a divine pleasure to admire, and that there are but few cities in Europe where the faculties of admiration can be so cultivated as in the grand old capital of Scotland. Whether it be antiquarian, romantic, picturesque, or scholarly, whatever is sought for, the tourist will find plenty of food in Edinburgh.

The city of itself has a population of two hundred and thirty-six thousand. While it is a seaport town, it seems to be dropped down upon the Highlands of Scotland, and has its ups and downs, and is very picturesque.

The first thing to attract your attention as you enter the city is the castle. This is a summit of rock some four hundred feet above the level of the sea. The top has a space of seven acres, and is a military fortress. It reminds one of the Acropolis of Athens. This place was used as a stronghold long before the authentic records of Scottish history; but none of the present buildings, with the exception of the little Norman chapel of Queen Margaret, date farther back than the fifteenth century. At one time it had a tower on it sixty feet high, called the tower of David II., erected about the year 1370.

In 1573 the gallant Kirkcaldy held the fortress for Queen Mary when it was attacked by Sir William Drury, who had five batteries playing on one point nine days, and David's tower was battered completely down, so that egress or ingress was impossible; and after thirty-three days the gallant Kirkcaldy surrendered, and had to be let down, he and his men, with ropes.

To-day the Highland laddies have their quarters there.

Calton Hill, farther north on a line with Prince Street, with an elevation of three hundred and forty feet above the sea, is another place of interest. On this is Dugald Stewart's monument and the royal observatory.

Here your curiosity will be excited when you see twelve stone columns forming the end of a building, looking like the Parthenon at Athens. You will ask some of the Scotch boys or girls that are playing about there the name of the structure, and they will say it is Edinburgh Folly. On further investigation we found that George IV. in 1822 commenced a monument to the Scotchmen that had fallen in the land and sea battles of Napoleon's time, and erected these twelve pillars at a cost of one thousand pounds each, when the funds gave out;

and there it stands as a curiosity of the nineteenth century.

The finest thing on this elevation is Nelson's monument, in circular form, one hundred and two feet high, with winding staircase inside, and battlemented summit, erected in 1815. On the flag-staff a huge ball is rigged, and is moved by mechanism adjusted to the observatory, that drops daily at one o'clock, Greenwich time, and communicates with and discharges instantaneously a gun at the castle. You can pay threepence, and go to the top of this monument, if you wish.

Scotland owes much to Sir Walter Scott. His Highland chief and other works have thrown a beautiful picture of Scotland broadcast to the world, and have attracted many tourists to the land so much admired by the great author.

In front of the Royal Hotel stands a beautiful monument, about two hundred feet high, costing some seventy-five thousand dollars, its cruciform, Gothic spire supported on four early English arches, which serve as a canopy for the marble statue of Sir Walter as he sits there upon a granite pedestal, with a book in his hand, and beside him lies his favorite dog, Maida. In the niches above the several arches are a great number of statuettes of leading characters of Scott's works, and there are many medallion likenesses of national poets.

I think the symmetry and beauty of this monument are wonderful. Every time I saw it I stopped and admired its beauty. The architect was a self-taught genius by the name of George Meikle Kemp, who was accidentally drowned in the Union Canal before this work was fully completed.

A little west of this monument is a bronze statue of Adam Black, Lord Provost and M.P. for the city, who was publisher of the Encyclopædia Britannica.

East, there are many other statues, those of Livingstone, Christopher North, Allan Ramsay, and Professor Simpson. These are all located in Prince Street Gardens, a beautiful place for a ramble at twilight, which at this season of the year in Edinburgh comes at a late hour. The chickens here retire about ten in the evening; and the mother can begin to scratch for them as early as three in the morning, if she wishes to do so. There are virtually only some four hours of darkness. In the winter this is reversed. Daylight is dealt out in small doses, darkness in quantity. The only objection to Edinburgh is that it is too near Norway, but I suppose our Scotch cousins think that what they lose in winter they make up in the summer.

Burns, the poet, spent much of his time here. It was also the home of John Knox, the great reformer. In the old part of the city you will see the house where he wrote the History of the Reformation. This is where he escaped the bullet of an assassin when it struck the candlestick before him, while he was sitting in meditation. It is said to be one of the oldest houses in the city. Knox died in this house in 1572, age sixty-seven. You will be shown a balcony where he used to stand and address the people. Near by the balcony are inscribed in Roman letters the first and second great commandments.

In Parliament Square you will see a small surface bronze stone in the ground, with the initials J. K. Here, Nov. 26, 1572, was placed all that was mortal of John Knox. The nobles and citizens were gathered there at that time, and Regent Morton pronounced over him a memorable eulogium, in which he used these words: "Here will rest the ashes of him who never feared the face of any man." Courage is one of the characteristics of the Scotch people. John Knox no doubt had his share.

The Mercat Cross, in one of the squares of Edinburgh, with its history, is worthy of your attention. It is as old as Edinburgh itself. It was destroyed in 1577; but in 1885, through the efforts of Mr. Gladstone, it was restored, and around it to-day are clustered the memories of perilous days. Here the citizens celebrated the accessions of all the Jameses, the blue blanket was unfurled, at the sound of the bells of St. Giles the burghers gathered to fight the English or to defend the town from hostile inroads. It was the place where the crier stood to proclaim the laws or sale of goods. James VI. and Charles I. endeavored here to impose laws which Scotland refused to obey. Charles II. followed in the same foolish way, and many victims of the persecuting times came to a martyr's crown at the cross.

The Holyrood Palace and chapel and Parliament Building are places of interest; but one of the largest buildings in Scotland is the Museum of Art and Science, four hundred feet long, two hundred feet wide, ninety feet high, lighted in the evening by horizontal rods in the roof, studded with gas-burners. The number of jets is five thousand.

You, no doubt, would enjoy staying longer in Edinburgh; but the wheels of time are moving rapidly, and we will take the train to-morrow morning for Melrose. About one and a half hours' ride will give us a delightful day.

SCOTLAND TO AMERICA.

Melrose is one of the delightful spots of Scotland; for I believe that Sir Walter Scott worshipped the god of nature, and his heart was full when he revelled in the beautiful scenery around Melrose. On arrival we will visit Melrose Abbey first. This is the ruin of an old church or convent.

They will show you the stone on which Sir Walter used to sit in meditation. Many of the rich and beautiful thoughts found in his works might have originated here.

After looking over this historical relic, we will engage a jolly Scotchman with his carriage to drive us to Abbotsford, some two and one-half miles, the home of Sir Walter Scott. Here you leave your carriage in the main road, take a pathway that leads down into a beautiful dell embowered with trees, and you soon see the home of Scott; and you will decide that the architect had a mind of his own, and has reared a building with some oddities, yet which, with its towers, angles, and surroundings, is a thing of beauty.

A little west of the house is the meandering brook with its silver stream as it goes rippling and singing its way onward. It is said that this little stream gave this noted Scotchman a great deal of enjoyment as he listened to its music wafted by the breeze to his library and study rooms where he spent so much of his time.

The place is owned by Sir Walter Scott's granddaughter, and is kept just as he left it, and must be yielding her a good return, as every one that enters pays an English shilling for the privilege. You will find a very pleasant young lady there that will show you through the house, giving all the information wished for; and it is a perfect museum of itself, filled with relics presented to the great author by kings, princes, and nobles.

Here you can look over his library of twenty thousand volumes, here you see his chair and desk just as he left them, also the last suit of clothes he wore, with his white stove-pipe hat, Scotch plaid trowsers, shoes, say No. 8, but with more breadth than length.

The swords and implements of war seem to have a large share in the exhibition. Whether this was Sir Walter's taste or the taste of his friends that presented them, I am not able to say, but am of the impression that the rod and gun, with his favorite dog, Maida, and in company with his Highland chief, Rob Roy, spending his leisure hours among the hills and valleys of Loch Katrine and Loch Lomond, is where Sir Walter found his enjoyment and recreation, and relief from hours of toil. Not only that, but in these simple amusements he found the inspiration that is seen in his works that we are enjoying to-day.

After drinking our fill of the scenes and surroundings of a lifetime, we will retrace our steps to the place where we left our carriage, and return to Melrose. We then drive to Dryburgh, some four miles, where rest the ashes of Sir Walter Scott and family.

After three-quarters of an hour's drive you will halt on the bank of a small river, where you find a suspension foot-bridge. You cross this, turn to your right, and a walk of twenty minutes, and you will find yourself in a meandering pathway, with the beautiful trees of Scotland all about you. You will say at once that this is a retreat for lovers; and you soon come to the ruins of an old abbey, in which is the tomb of Sir Walter and others.

The keeper of the place will tell you that Scott used to spend hours in this retreat with his wife, when she was his best girl; and no doubt it became one of the dearest spots on earth to him, and was probably the reason why his earth's journey was ended here.

As the sun seems to be dropping down in the western sky, we will return to Melrose and take the train for Edinburgh, where we spend the night, and take an early start in the morning, June 28, for Glasgow, going through the Trossachs. The train leaves about eight in the morning. So we have time for breakfast, and bid our cousins at Edinburgh good-by, and receive a cordial invitation to come again, to which our hearts say Yea and Amen.

Our train is soon sweeping us through the beautiful scenery of Scotland. We go through Sterling, a place of beauty, with its ruined castle, where we might spend a day with profit; but time is limited, and we pass on to where we leave the train at Callander, taking coaches for Loch Katrine, some half-mile or more this side of the boat landing. We stop at the charming Hotel Trossachs for lunch; and, if you have the time, it will pay you to stop over a day.

Good fishing is near at hand, the scenery delightful, the hotel the personification of neatness, the cuisine excellent. But our coach is ready, and we bid good-by to one of the loveliest spots in Scotland, and go to the landing, where we find "Rob Roy" waiting for us.

This is a nice little skipper, and will carry some seventy-five persons, if necessary, and is a much better boat in fair than foul weather. But we were fortunate, it being one of June's bright, charming days; and all went merry as a marriage bell.

Probably Loch Katrine and her surroundings were never more charming in appearance than this day that we saw her. If you are expecting to see high and rugged mountains along her shores, you will be disappointed. The highest elevation is only little more than a thousand feet.

This, to a New Englander, is rather a tame affair; but, like Lake George, the scenery fills your soul with admiration. The shores are not abrupt, but gradually recede, with foliage to the top of the hills; and in many places the slopes are so gradual that the Highlanders have their dwellings near the shore, with their fields and flocks climbing back upon the mountains.

There seems to be a great variety of trees and foliage upon these mountains, which give different shades of coloring. This, as you go sailing down the lake, passing Ellen Isle and Silver Strand, will give you a charming picture. "Rob Roy" is about one and one-half hours in reaching Stronach Lochar, near the lower end of the lake, where we find coaches to take us to Inversnaid, where we take a larger steamer on the waters of Loch Lomond.

Loch Katrine was the little sister with her coquettish beauty. Loch Lomond is more stately and dignified, but comely in appearance. At Inversnaid there is a fine hotel; but we had satisfied the inner man at the Hotel Trossachs. Therefore, we spent our time in admiring the beauties of Inversnaid and surroundings, which is near the upper end of Loch Lomond.

In some forty-five minutes after our arrival by coach we find ourselves on board of a very comfortable steamer, with her prow headed down the lake, commencing a three hours' ride for the lower end of the lake, where we take a car-ride of twenty miles to Glasgow.

As we pursued our journey, we found the lake somewhat narrow, giving us beautiful scenery on our right; and on our left we passed Rob Roy's cave, also his prison where he held his victims until he secured ransom money. You will see at our left where the city of Glasgow has tunnelled under the mountains, and taken their supply of water, a distance of thirty-four miles, costing millions.

Queen Victoria attended the opening of this great enterprise. Farther on Ben Lomond looms up to a height of over three thousand feet, and is the Mount Washington of that region. Birch, ash, oak, and in many places the heather cover the sides of the hills and mountains with charming effect. As we pass on the last hour of our sail, Loch Lomond is much wider and filled with beautiful islands. About four o'clock we tie up at the pier, and take a train for Glasgow, reaching our hotel at half-past five.

June 27, Thursday morning, we start out to investigate Glasgow, a city of five hundred thousand inhabitants, with suburbs of nearly another half million. The Clyde passes through the city. This river is the promoter of Glasgow, or, if you prefer, you can call Glasgow the offspring of the Clyde.

It is the great ship-building port of the world. The river is not wide, but is deep, so they can slide in the largest boats that plough the ocean, and steam them down into the Atlantic. We will now step on board a small steamer that plies up and down the Clyde, and go down the river some five miles. On your right and left the staging poles and masts look like a forest; and, when you hear the clanging of hammers and chisels upon the heavy steel plates as they are being fitted, you will decide at once that the man that can make the most noise is the best fellow, and that every man's effort is crowned with success.

We pass the yard where they have been and are building yachts that have competed, and are to continue to compete, for the national cup. We also pass the abattoir where they butcher nothing but American cattle.

Before they turned the prow of the steamer up the river, they pointed out to us the town of Paisley, where the famous Paisley shawls originated; but the day of that article has gone by, and they are making other goods now.

But what will surprise you in taking this trip is the hundreds of acres of ship-yards on the banks of the Clyde. This has brought in an immense amount of money, and made Glasgow what she is to-day, the great manufacturing city of Scotland.

The sewerage of the city empties into the Clyde, and the impurities are making them trouble; and they are devising ways to take care of it elsewhere, which will be a blessing to those that are on or near the river.

We enjoyed our stay in Glasgow, though it was a short one, leaving in the afternoon for Manchester, where we spent the night, going through to London the next day, feeling that our trip to Scotland was a decided success.

Saturday night found us nicely located and everything in running order at the Hotel Metropole in London.

Sunday we go to hear Joseph Parker preach his twenty-fifth anniversary sermon, also to Westminster Abbey to hear Canon Farrar. There it was Flower Sunday, and children took part in the services, and everything was in keeping with the flowery kingdom. Monday morning we will put in an appearance there again, as you will find it an immense building and a perfect burying-ground of itself; and whoever preaches there preaches to the dead and the living,— which class is the best listeners is a question.

The crypt is full of dead men's bones; and the main part is the last resting-place of many heroes, princes, and nobles. You will see many inscriptions speaking of their honors and gallant deeds. One of the honored ones fell at Ticonderoga. Perhaps Ethan Allen could give us the circumstances. Westminster Abbey is old and honored, and is one of the great attractions of London.

From here you had better go to St. Paul's cathedral. There is the last resting-place of the late General Gordon. Many a noted man in silent manner will speak to you there, and you will be interested in hunting for the heroes of olden times.

The architecture of this building is grand. You can revel in churches in London any length of time if your taste runs that way.

But you may weary of these things; and we will take up temporal and material things, and go to the Bank of England, the great financial institution of London. There you will see them dropping the bags of gold into strong boxes, strapped with iron, then lifted with blocks and pulleys to a platform, where they are shipped to the four corners of the earth. They informed us that the week before they had shipped twenty-five million to France. They seem to be doing business on a large scale. You will see every day late in the afternoon one hundred or more soldiers marching from the barracks to the bank, and they remain in and on top of the building through the night.

From here you can go to the Thames. This will give you an idea of the manufacturing of London, which is located on the banks of this river.

Then go some eight miles up the Thames, and you reach Hampton Court, where you can visit the

ONE OF "THE BEEF EATERS."

palace with all its fine paintings, and see the regal splendor of the kings, see one of the largest grapevines in the world with its twenty-five hundred bunches of grapes to tempt your palate, also a wistaria of about the same proportion.

From there take a carriage, and drive through the two-thousand-acre park, strewn with English oaks and beeches and a variety of trees with beautiful deer seen in all directions. In going through this park,˙ you will visit the mammoth conservatories, with tropical plants and flowers in great variety.

You can return to your hotel by rail or boat, as you may choose. You are probably weary, as all sight-seers usually are when the shades of eve close in upon them.

We shall want to go to the Tower and prison, and see the relics and implements of execution and torture of olden times.

In that section of London you see the beef-eaters, with their pleated bell-topped hats and peculiar dress. These are the old retired soldiers, and it is considered quite an honor for the queen to send one of these men with you on any expedition.

The British Museum is extensive, filled with sketches, Indian relics, etc.. The historical take the lead.

But if you wish for the beautiful in painting and sculpture, productions of the great artists, then go to Kensington Museum, which is some twenty minutes from Trafalgar Square by bus or hansom. The latter are charming to ride in. They all have rubber tires; and you hear nothing but the horses' feet as they go clipping over the pavement, which is usually of excellent quality.

A trip to Windsor Castle will be in order. A drive to Hyde Park, and take in on our way Prince Albert's monument, which was, from appearance, patterned after Sir Walter Scott's at Edinburgh, perhaps a little more elaborate, but of the same general appearance. Prince Albert sitting there in his royal apparel and gold lace is more attractive than Scott with his Highland plaid trousers and coat to match. But Sir Walter may live as long in the hearts of the people as the other man.

Next let us look at the London Bridge across the Thames, where the poet stood at midnight, when the clock was striking the hour, and the moon shone over the city, etc.

The Houses of Parliament were erected in 1840 from a plan by Sir Charles Barry, which was selected from ninety-seven sent in for competition. Of Gothic style, it covers an area of eight acres, contains eleven courts, one hundred staircases, and eleven hundred apartments, and cost £3,000,000. It is situated on the Thames, and the basement is said to be lower than the river at high water. The Clock Tower, at the north end next to Westminster Bridge, is three hundred and eighteen feet high, the Middle Tower is three hundred feet high, and the south-west, Victoria Tower, the largest of the three, through which the queen enters when opening Parliament, attains a height of three hundred and forty feet. This building carries an immense clock, with faces twenty-three feet in diameter. It takes five hours to wind up the striking parts. A light in the Clock Tower by night and the royal standard flying on Victoria Tower by day indicate that Parliament is in session.

In the Clock Tower is one of the largest bells known, which is called "Big Ben." It weighs thirteen tons, and can be heard all over London. The inside of this building is rich and imposing, and one can have the privilege of passing through it on Saturdays from ten to four. You enter on the west side, by a door adjacent to Victoria Tower. Policemen are stationed in every room; and they hurry you through, merely giving a chance for a glimpse at the regal splendor as you pass along. As you enter, you pass through the Norman Porch, or hall. Turning to the right, you enter the queen's robing-room, forty-five feet long, beautifully decorated, and containing beautiful paintings, the state chair, etc., which will stir the admiration of every one. Next comes the Royal or Victoria Gallery, one hundred and ten feet long. Through this room the queen proceeds as she goes from the robing-room in solemn procession to the House of Peers to open Parliament.

On leaving this gallery, you enter the prince's chamber, a smaller apartment, but of simple magnificence, being decorated with dark wood, for which the Middle Ages were famous.

Here the stained-glass windows exhibit the rose, thistle, and shamrock, emblems of England, Scotland, and Ireland. From here you can enter the House of Peers, which is ninety feet by forty-five, and forty-five feet high. The floor is largely occupied with long leather-covered benches, sufficient to seat five hundred and fifty members.

In this room is the throne, covered with its richly gilded canopy. Here also you will see twelve stained-glass windows, containing the portraits of the kings and queens of England since the Conquest. At night the house is lighted from outside through these windows.

This room, with its throne and paraphernalia for the kings, queens, and lords of the nation, is superior to the House of Commons, which you will pass through before leaving the building. The central hall will attract your attention. It is in the centre of the building, octagonal in shape, sixty feet in diameter, and seventy-five feet high, and richly decorated. Here you will see Venetian mosaics, and glass mosaic finishing, and fittings in keeping with the nation it represents.

From here you can go to Westminster Hall, where you can leave the building with a feeling that you have walked the floor that has been trodden by mental giants, lords, kings, and queens of the land.

We have enjoyed our trip to Scotland and our stay in London much more than we expected, but our friends in Vermont are waiting our arrival; and we will take passage on the "Lahn" July 3, leaving London at 10 A.M., with a run of two hours to Southampton, where we are put on to a lighter and run out into the bay, and transferred to our steamer of the German Lloyd line, not as large as the "Normannia," that took us out on our tour, but a boat we like quite as well.

The English Channel was remarkably civil to us, letting us out on to the broad ocean without stirring up any bad blood or anything else unpleasant.

The next day, the Fourth, was, of course, a memorable day to every American ; and, from the general appearance of the passengers, many were from that land.

While our captain and crew were Germans, they were remarkably civil and mindful of the Americans.

In the morning we found the dining-room decorated with the stars and stripes. The band through the day played the national airs. At 6 P.M. we had a course dinner. On the menu was illuminated ice cream, U.S.A. Near the close of the feast the curtains were drawn at the windows, the electric lights were turned off, and in came the stewards and the waiters holding a receptacle or platter up as high as their heads, with an inverted glass dish on it with a light inside. Around this sat little Dutchmen, Yankees, and Japanese made of ice-cream, holding little flags of the stars and stripes, little umbrellas, etc. The marching was up and down, back and forth among the tables, until the waiters had covered the whole hall. Of course, we Americans saw the point, and cheered them lustily. It was certainly a unique celebration to every one.

We had only two days of rough sailing, with racks on the tables ; half day and night of fog, when we had the pleasure of listening to the music of the fog-horn ; encountered no icebergs, and only one whale. He saluted us by throwing water some twenty feet into the air, and then went on his way, and we did ours. On the whole, it was a very satisfactory passage, sailing July 3, reaching quarantine in the evening of the 10th, landing early in the morning of the 11th, being five months, less two days, from the time the "Normannia" swung from her pier and headed her prow down North River, with the Oriental party on board with high expectations, which have been more than realized, being watched over by a kind Providence, giving a joyful experience and safe return to our native heath, stronger, truer Americans than ever.

USEFUL HINTS FOR TRAVELLERS.

Those who have never crossed the ocean and travelled in foreign countries would, no doubt, like a short chapter with a few suggestions as to preparations for the journey and what to do after you weigh anchor. First as to luggage and clothing: unless you have friends and acquaintances among the royal blood in the old country, you had better leave laces, frills, and fine jewelry at home; for you will probably not have a chance to go on dress parade until you return to America. Take strong, servicable clothing, with easy fitting and strong foot-gear.

You should prepare for the heat and cold. This can be done largely with underclothing, and this will enable you to bring your baggage into a small compass and light weight. Fifty-six pounds in the old country is about the amount that goes through without extra charge. Then the custom-house officers are always suspicious of large trunks, and will give the owners of such more or less annoyance. A fair amount of linen is desirable, though there is no trouble in getting washing done in almost any city you may stop in. Celluloid collars and cuffs for gentlemen are a fine thing, as they can be cleaned at any time, and will reduce the washing bill.

Follow the above, and you will have no trouble in arranging your wardrobe. I am indebted to a lady for the following suggestions in regard to articles most needed. A serge or similar dress of wool is suitable for ocean and ordinary travel, the skirt made of short walking length. The present fashion of skirt and fancy waists seems to supply a variety of costumes for all seasons without increasing the baggage much, one black silk answering where more dress is required; and, with a few fresh laces and ribbons, one can make quite a smart appearance. For the donkey riding in Egypt, a mohair dress would be desirable, as it easily sheds dust. If partly worn, it will be good enough. A common divided skirt or equestrian tights or both are quite desirable; a straw hat, with a sash (called a puggery) of light silk or lawn fastened around it, falling in the back to protect the back of the head and neck from the sun; also a large, light gauze veil to protect the face from the dust and flies.

A white parasol or small umbrella lined with green is almost a necessity, and can be easily carried while riding. Carry several pairs of partly worn kid gloves. This costume will be equally suitable for horseback riding through Palestine, with the addition of a water-proof and rubbers. The white parasol is a good protection from the sudden showers which often greet one in passing over the mountains of Lebanon. Do not fail to have an unlined flannel wrapper, which can be worn over the ordinary night clothing. It is necessary for the camping, and will be found very comfortable in most hotels and on the steamers.

The common crocheted slippers should also be

a part of the wardrobe; for throughout Syria the floors are mostly of stone or cement, and sometimes there are no rugs.

A yard of common white lace will be found very desirable as a screen from flies, etc., if one would take a nap in comfort on the Nile.

The great bugbear is seasickness, which is the oldest and yet the most modern disease we know anything about. Its symptoms, effects, and results are probably the same now as they were when Jonah shipped from Jaffa to Tarshish. Jonah was not a sailor; and, when the ocean became so rough, he no doubt was seasick in his bunk, and did not care a picayune whether they threw him overboard or not. It seems that the whale that swallowed him caught the disease, and threw up Jonah after three days,—the only case of contagion we know of. The stomach seems to be the troublesome member; and, if you could leave it at home or put it in your trunk, there would be but little trouble in crossing the ocean.

The number of remedies is great; and, whichever one you take, you are liable to wish you had taken the other. Drinking mineral water with lemon in it a few days before sailing is said to be a preventive. Put a capsicum plaster on the pit of the stomach the day you sail. This I believe to be as good a remedy as can be found. Bromide of soda is another panacea, and no doubt a good one. You had better take with you a rubber hot-water bottle and a small medicine chest, with laxatives, astringents, remedies for colds and fever attacks,—these not especially for the ocean voyage, but to have with you in all your travels. However, the best remedy is, take care of yourself, and make up your mind that you are not going to be sick, certainly so when on the ocean. Stay on deck, pay but little attention to the sea, whether smooth or rough, be indifferent as possible to that part of your surroundings; and, if you have to feed the fishes, go to the leeward side of the boat, and not to the windward. If you find the waves are getting the upper hand of you, then take to your berth, and keep on your back until the sea becomes smooth.

Occasionally you will find persons that have to stay in their berth the whole sea voyage, but these are rare cases. The crews that man our ocean steamers are, as a rule, very polite and attentive, and of course expect to receive tips, which should not be given until the last day. Common fees are as follows: bedroom steward, $2; two table waiters, $1.25 each; the stewardess, $1, unless you have to call on her often, then pay according to services rendered; deck steward, $1, unless you need extra attention, then you will desire to give him more.

You had better secure your steamer chair, if you wish for any, as soon as you go aboard, rental $1 each. If they have a band, as they probably will, you will be asked to contribute for that. As to the amount, you will be governed by the ear for music you may have. So you see it will be an easy matter to get rid of eight or ten dollars, although there is no compulsion in any of these tips; but a person who wishes to take a foreign trip and get along without tips had better wear a coat of mail, and expect to receive the anathema of all the waiters of a foreign land. Tips in the Old World are the custom. The waiters work for low wages or none at all; and, if they are polite and attentive, I enjoy seeing them have a few loose shillings about them when I bid them good-by. Cook & Sons and Henry Gaze & Sons are the two old established firms of tourist agents in the old country, and are very reliable firms. Raymond & Whitcomb have recently commenced tours abroad. Their service in this country has been excellent, none better to travel with. These firms usually charge about $10 a day, but you are relieved of all care and anxiety. A small party can go independently, and hire their guide when and wherever they may need one, as they can be found in any country, price from two to four dollars per day. This divided among six or eight amounts to but a trifle. In that way a party can travel for six or seven dollars per day; and you can be quite independent, stay as long or as short a time in a place as you please. If you have some in your party that can speak French or German, it will help you wonderfully. Have your passport, and with your letter of credit you can get English or French gold, which is good in any country.

The money of the country you are in you should get rid of before leaving that country to enter another. If there is no other way, and you have your wife with you, hand it to her; for she will very quickly find curiosities and articles you will like to bring home with you, which will soon clean out the loose change you may have about you. Heavy overcoats for gentlemen taking a sea voyage are the things to have, and fur cloaks and steamer rugs for ladies. Below you will find the denominations of money of different countries, giving their value in American coin, which will be well for any one to study that is going into those countries. Many people are exceedingly afraid of drinking the water in a foreign land. There may be those that enjoy that delusion for the sake of an excuse to drink wine and beer; but there are many that would prefer the water if it could be taken with safety; and there is no doubt that it can be, certainly in a hilly country. Use your own judgment in the matter. When you think there is danger, drink tea or coffee or water that has been boiled; and your countenance will be more charming than it would have been, had you confined yourself to the wine and beer of the land. Regarding hotel carriages, drives, donkey rides, etc., always make your contracts beforehand.

German coin.	U.S. coin.	Turkish coin.	U.S. coin.
Carolin	$4.92	Asper ($\frac{1}{120}$ piastre)	
Groschen ($\frac{1}{30}$ thaler)	.02⅓	Beshlik (5 piastres)	$0.21
Heller (1 pfennig)	.00¼	Lira (100 piastres)	4.40
Kreutzer ($\frac{1}{30}$ mark)	.00⅔	Medjidie (20 piastres)	.88
Krone (10 marks)	2.38	Piastre	.04
Mark (100 pfennigs)	.24¼	Purse (500 piastres)	21.73
Thaler (3 marks)	.71½	Shereefee	227.00

English coin.	U.S. coin.	Italian coin.	U.S. coin.
Pound (20 shillings)	$4.85	Marengo (20 francs)	$3.86
Crown (5 shillings)	1.21	Scudo (5 lire)	.97
Florin (2 shillings)	.48½	Lire (100 centimes)	.19½
Guinea (21 shillings)	5.09¼	Soldo ($\frac{1}{20}$ lire)	.01
Penny ($\frac{1}{12}$ shilling)	.02	Testone	.32
Shilling (12 pence)	.24		

French coin.	U.S. coin.
Centime ($\frac{1}{100}$ franc)	$0.00⅕
Decime ($\frac{1}{10}$ franc)	.02
Franc	.19½
Sou ($\frac{1}{20}$ franc)	.01

www.ingramcontent.com/pod-product-compliance
Lightning Source LLC
Chambersburg PA
CBHW020805230426
43666CB00007B/868